Bugopedia

THE COMPLETE GUIDE TO EVERYTHING INSECT

Plus Other Creepy-Crawlies

With an introduction by entomologist Brendan Dunphy

American giant cockroach

Time HOME ENTERTAINMENT

Publisher: Margot Schupf
Vice President, Finance: Vandana Patel
Executive Director, Marketing Services: Carol Pittard
Executive Director, Business Development: Suzanne Albert
Executive Director, Marketing: Susan Hettleman
Publishing Director: Megan Pearlman
Associate Director of Publicity: Courtney Greenhalgh
Assistant General Counsel: Simone Procas
Assistant Director, Special Sales: Ilene Schreider
Assistant Director, Finance: Christine Font
Senior Manager, Sales Marketing: Danielle Costa
Senior Manager, Children's Category Marketing: Amanda Lipnick
Associate Production Manager: Kimberly Marshall
Associate Prepress Manager: Alex Voznesenskiy
Associate Project Manager: Stephanie Braga

Editorial Director: Stephen Koepp
Art Director: Gary Stewart
Senior Editors: Roe D'Angelo, Alyssa Smith
Managing Editor: Matt DeMazza
Editor, Children's Books: Jonathan White
Copy Chief: Rina Bander
Design Manager: Anne-Michelle Gallero
Assistant Managing Editor: Gina Scauzillo
Editorial Assistant: Courtney Mifsud

Special Thanks: Allyson Angle, Katherine Barnet, Brad Beatson,
Jeremy Biloon, John Champlin, Ian Chin, Susan Chodakiewicz,
Rose Cirrincione, Tracy Conner, Assu Etsubneh, Mariana Evans,
Alison Foster, Kristina Jutzi, David Kahn, Jean Kennedy, Hillary Leary,
Samantha Long, Amy Mangus, Robert Martells, Nina Mistry, Sue Perez-
Jackson, Melissa Presti, Danielle Prielipp, Kate Roncinske, Babette Ross,
Dave Rozzelle, Matthew Ryan, Ricardo Santiago, Divyam Shrivastava

Published by Time Home Entertainment Inc.
1271 Avenue of the Americas, 6th floor • New York, NY 10020

ISBN 10: 1-60320-988-3
ISBN 13: 978-1-60320-988-5

We welcome your comments and suggestions about
Time Home Entertainment books. Please write to us at:
**Time Home Entertainment books, Attention: Book Editors,
P.O. Box 361095, Des Moines, IA 50336-1095**

If you would like to order any of our hardcover Collector's Edition
books, please call us at 800-327-6388, Monday through Friday,
7 a.m.–9 p.m., Central Time.

Produced by **SCOUT** BOOKS&MEDIA

President: Susan Knopf
Writer: James Buckley, Jr.
Special Advisor: Brendan Dunphy, entomologist
Editor: Beth Sutinis
Copyeditor: Stephanie Engel
Assistant Editor and Photo Research: Brittany Gialanella
Designed by: Andrij Borys Associates, LLC
Designers: Andrij Borys and Iwona Usakiewicz
Associate Designers: Mia Balaquiot and Jessica Rizzo
Special Thanks: Chelsea Burris, Michael Centore

*Ant and aphid
in garden*

ABOUT THIS BOOK

Numbering more than a million species, insects make up the largest group of animals on Earth. In *Bugopedia*, you'll meet hundreds and hundreds of them. Though most insects are small, they play a huge part in our world. Without insects, we might not have food to eat, and animals that eat insects would go hungry. Earth would be filled with rotting plants and garbage. Insects help us with everything from making clothing to solving crimes.

Inside this book, you'll find out how insects around the globe live, eat, and move. See how they connect to humans in hundreds of ways. Also, learn how insects go through amazing transformations. Every page has cool information about the world of insects and other arthropods, such as spiders, scorpions, and centipedes. *Bugopedia* will show you how other arthropods are similar to and different from insects and explain their roles within our ecosystem.

To guide your reading, look for a few special features. Bug behavior boxes highlight fascinating ways that insects live their lives. "WORD" introduces key terms used by scientists and other experts. "ON THE FLY!" tells stories of insects in the news, while "EUREKA!" describes key insect discoveries.

Another feature you'll find is "BRENDAN SAYS." That's where you'll read inside information from Brendan Dunphy, the *Bugopedia* entomology expert. An entomologist is someone who studies insects, and Brendan has been obsessed with them since he was a kid. He works with insects every day at his job at Iowa State University and has hosted TV shows and specials about these amazing animals.

One thing Brendan wants readers to know is that the world of insects is always changing. You'll see numbers inside that say how many species of a particular type of insect live in the world. Those numbers are always going up as scientists travel around finding new insects. Keep in mind that many insect species look similar to one another. Sometimes it's impossible to know from a photograph whether an insect is species A, B, or C. We tried hard to get them all right.

You can read *Bugopedia* in any order you want. We suggest taking a look at the information at the front of the book first. That section talks about what makes an insect an insect and how insects are placed in orders and families. The chapters are arranged according to those orders. Finally, at the back, you'll find information on how to track down even more facts and news about insects, and definitely check out the activities that you and your friends can do together to learn about insects.

Contents

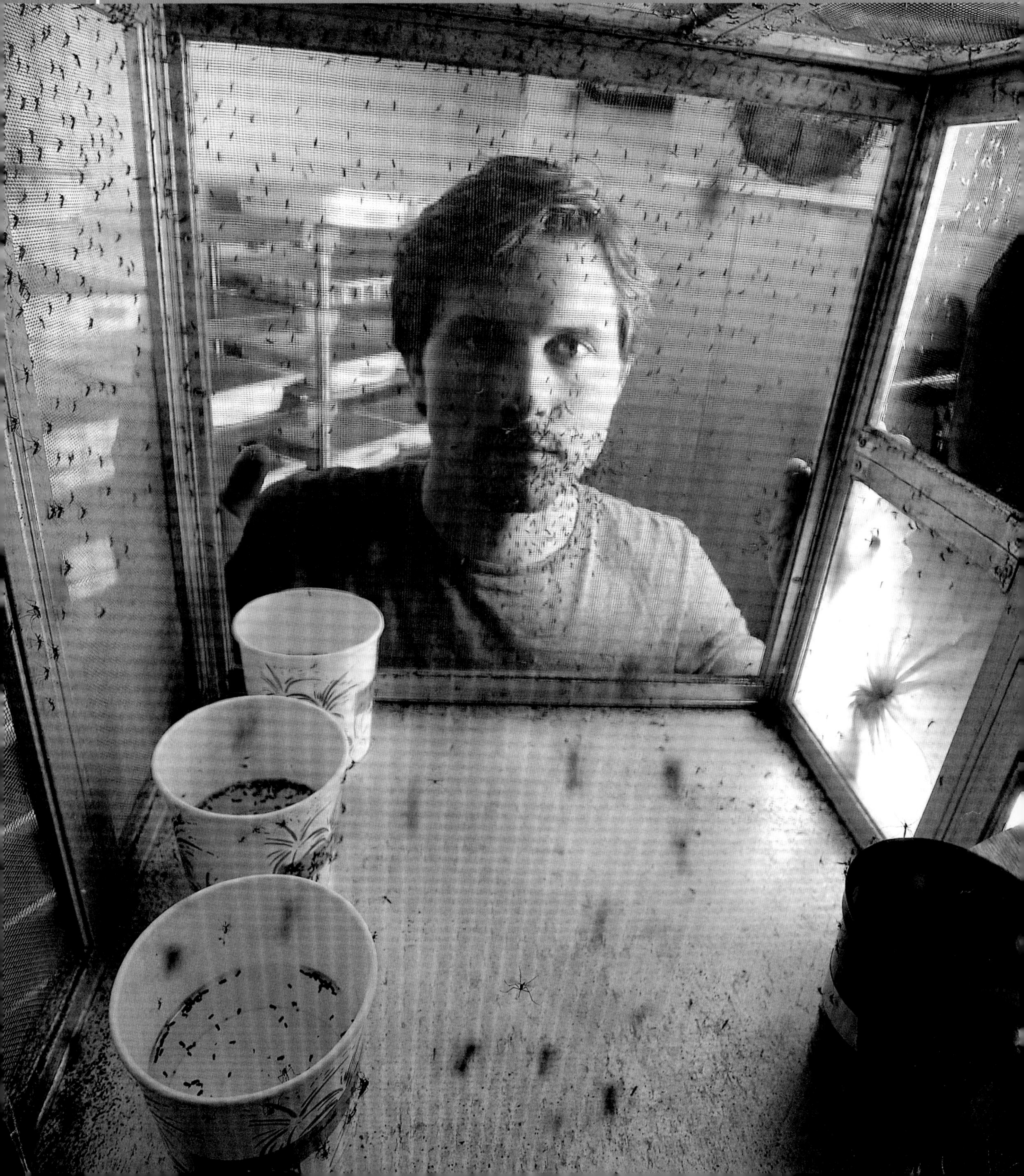

A lot of people say that insects are creepy, crawly, scary, and gross. But I disagree. I think insects are AMAZING! I have enjoyed every minute of my many years studying these creatures, and I learn something new every day. Insects have adapted to live just about everywhere on Earth, in a spectacular variety of sizes, shapes, colors, and forms. They have evolved to live, grow, feed, and move in ways that are endlessly fascinating. It sometimes seems that the things they are doing are not even possible. Insects are almost like comic-book superheroes (and sometimes super villains!).

Insects are my passion now, but I've always loved animals of all sorts. My mom likes to tell the story of how I caught a cricket when I was just a toddler. Instead of squishing it, I put my hand over it, and I laughed each time I lifted my hand and it leaped away. Later, when we lived in Louisiana, I caught a coral snake and carried it around the neighborhood in a soda bottle. (Kids: Do NOT try this at home—coral snakes are dangerous!) I was a regular visitor to local zoos, and I spent time in the woods catching crayfish and frogs. I even became an active bird-watcher.

I knew I wanted to work with animals for a career, so I went to Iowa State University expecting to become a veterinarian—an animal doctor. But I ended up studying zoology instead. Being a zoology major was great because zoologists learn about the entire animal kingdom—everything from the tiniest creatures to the most massive, from the molecules that make up their bodies to the ways they interact with their environments. While I was in college, I took trips to Africa to study animals. I worked on a project that helped turtles in Massachusetts. And I dug into the ground looking for fossils of long-ago invertebrates (animals without backbones). Working in the field and being outdoors observing animals are some of the most fun things about being a zoologist.

Eventually, I decided to focus on entomology, the study of insects. Since then, I have never tired of learning more about them. There are so many species of insect to study that you could become an expert in one area but know nothing about a million other species. Even in my specialty, mosquitoes, there is so much to learn. For instance, I've gotten to know the 55 species of mosquito in Iowa really well, but that is just a tiny, tiny, tiny drop in the bucket of what there is to know about mosquitoes.

Many people are indeed afraid of insects. It's time to change that—and you can help. After you read *Bugopedia*, spread the word. Insects are a vital part of our world; we might not even be alive without some kinds of insects. They help the plants that we eat grow, for example. Some insects become food for people to eat. Some insects are studied to find out more about genetics and other parts of science. Insects eat other insects that are not as friendly to our plants. And who can imagine a world without the beauty of butterflies?

If you're looking to jump into the world of insects with all six legs, *Bugopedia* is a great place to start. The photos draw you in, the words explain things, and the whole experience will lead you to new and amazing insect discoveries.

Read on and enjoy!

Brendan Dunphy

Brendan Dunphy
Entomologist

Organizing the Bugs

Experts use scientific names for animals so that, no matter where they live or what language they speak, they can be certain they are referring to the same species. An animal's scientific name is a combination of two parts: the genus and the species. For example, a particular type of butterfly is named *Danaus plexippus*. *Danaus* is the genus name for tiger butterflies, and *plexippus* is the specific species. Most people know this insect by its common name, the monarch butterfly. However, with so many animals in the world, only a small percentage of them have been given common names. This book features animals that do have common names. You'll learn about insects, arachnids, millipedes, and centipedes—all part of the large group of animals called arthropods.

SCIENTIFIC NAMING SYSTEM FOR ANIMALS

Kingdom	The world of living things is divided into five kingdoms: animals, bacteria, plants, fungi, and protists (which are microorganisms).	Insects are part of the animal kingdom.
Phylum (FYE-luhm)	This section separates animals into groups with major shared traits, such as having a backbone or not. Animals with backbones are vertebrates. Those without, such as insects, are invertebrates.	Insects, arachnids, centipedes, and millipedes are invertebrates that all have exoskeletons and limbs with several joints each. This puts them together in the phylum Arthropoda.
Class	Phyla (the plural of phylum) are further divided into classes of related animals.	Insects are in the class Insecta. Spiders, which are also arthropods, are in Arachnida.
Order	Animals that look alike and have similar features? They'll be put in the same order. Orders can be further broken into suborders. And some orders are combined into superorders. In this book, most insects are presented in their superorders.	Insecta includes 29 orders. Beetles are part of Coleoptera, for example. Butterflies are part of Lepidoptera. Arachnida includes ten+ orders.
Family	Animals with more and more shared traits are gathered into families.	How many insect families are there? Most experts agree that there are about 800. There are only about 100 spider families, in comparison.
Genus (JEE-nuhs)	A genus gathers up animals that are very similar in many ways.	Among the 800 insect families, there are tens of thousands of insect genera (the plural of genus).
Species	Each genus is made up of different species. The animals in a species are able to breed with one another and reproduce.	

More than 200 years ago, a Swedish scientist named Carl Linnaeus came up with a system. His system, called taxonomy, sorts living things into a series of related groups that get smaller and more specifically related until each animal is named as a unique species.

MILLIPEDES

Millipedes have more legs than any other animal on Earth. There are 7,753 millipede species, though only a few are seen regularly by people.

Kingdom: Animalia
Phylum: Arthropoda
Class: Diplopoda

INSECTS

With more than 1 million species, this is the largest class of animals in the world, comprising about half of all known species of living things. They all have at least one thing in common: six legs. There are 29 insect orders and about 800 families.

Kingdom: Animalia
Phylum: Arthropoda
Class: Insecta

ARACHNIDS

Spiders are the best-known members of this class; there are more than 40,000 spider species. Other members of this group include scorpions, ticks, mites, and harvestmen. One big difference from insects: These animals have eight legs.

Kingdom: Animalia
Phylum: Arthropoda
Class: Arachnida

CENTIPEDES

Their name hints that each animal has 100 legs, but most have far fewer. Like their fellow arthropods, centipedes have exoskeletons and are born out of eggs. There are 3,149 named species crawl around the globe.

Kingdom: Animalia
Phylum: Arthropoda
Class: Chilopoda

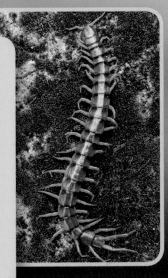

Honeypot ant

Insects

We are outnumbered. If scientists are right, there are more than 1.3 billion insects on Earth for every human being. It sounds like we need to know a lot more about insects. Read on!

AT A GLANCE

How do you keep track of more than a million different species of insects around the world? You name them, organize them into groups, and make a list. Scientists use groups to help organize insects… and so does *Bugopedia*. Insects are organized into groups throughout the book. You'll find these scientific names and their more familiar common names throughout the book.

Scientific Name	Common Name
Collembola	Springtails
Zygentoma	Silverfish
Ephemeroptera	Mayflies
Odonata	Dragonflies and damselflies
Isoptera	Termites
Blattodea	Cockroaches
Mantodea	Mantises
Phasmatodea	Stick and leaf insects
Orthoptera	Grasshoppers and crickets
Phthiraptera	Lice
Hemiptera	True bugs and others
Neuroptera	Lacewings and others
Coleoptera	Beetles
Diptera	Flies
Siphonaptera	Fleas
Lepidoptera	Butterflies and moths
Hymenoptera	Ants, bees, wasps, and others

The Mighty Exoskeleton

An insect does not have bones inside its body, as vertebrate animals do. Instead, the outside of its body is what holds it together. This is called an exoskeleton.

Rhinoceros beetle

BABY INSECTS

After coming out of their eggs, different species of insects live the first parts of their lives in different forms.

Some baby flies start out as limbless blobs called maggots.

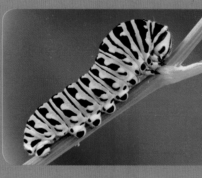

Beautiful butterflies grow from caterpillars.

Dragonfly babies live underwater before emerging into the air to live their adult lives.

There is a vast number of insect species, with enormous variety between them. However, all insects have some similar body parts. All insects have exoskeletons. And most insects have two or more separate time periods in their life cycles, meaning they may look different depending on their ages.

GROWING AND CHANGING

As insects grow, they molt, or shed their exoskeletons. During this process, the exoskeleton cracks and the insect climbs out, leaving behind a shell of its former self.

WORD

The prefix *exo-* means "outer," so an **exoskeleton** is a supportive structure on the outer part of the body. An endoskeleton, what a vertebrate has, is the opposite.

Adult insects come in many shapes and sizes, to say nothing of colors. But nearly all have some version of these basic anatomical parts.

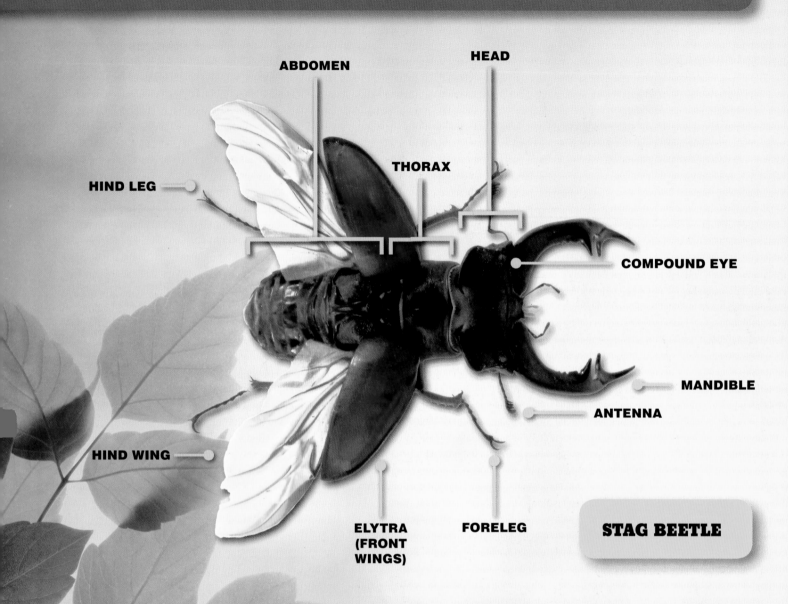

ABDOMEN

HEAD

THORAX

HIND LEG

COMPOUND EYE

MANDIBLE

ANTENNA

HIND WING

ELYTRA (FRONT WINGS)

FORELEG

STAG BEETLE

IN FLIGHT

Nearly all insects have wings and can fly at some stages of their lives. On dragonflies, for instance, the wings stick out to the sides. Most other winged insects can fold their wings backward over their abdomens. Beetles can fold their hind wings, used for flying, underneath forewings, which are hardened for protection.

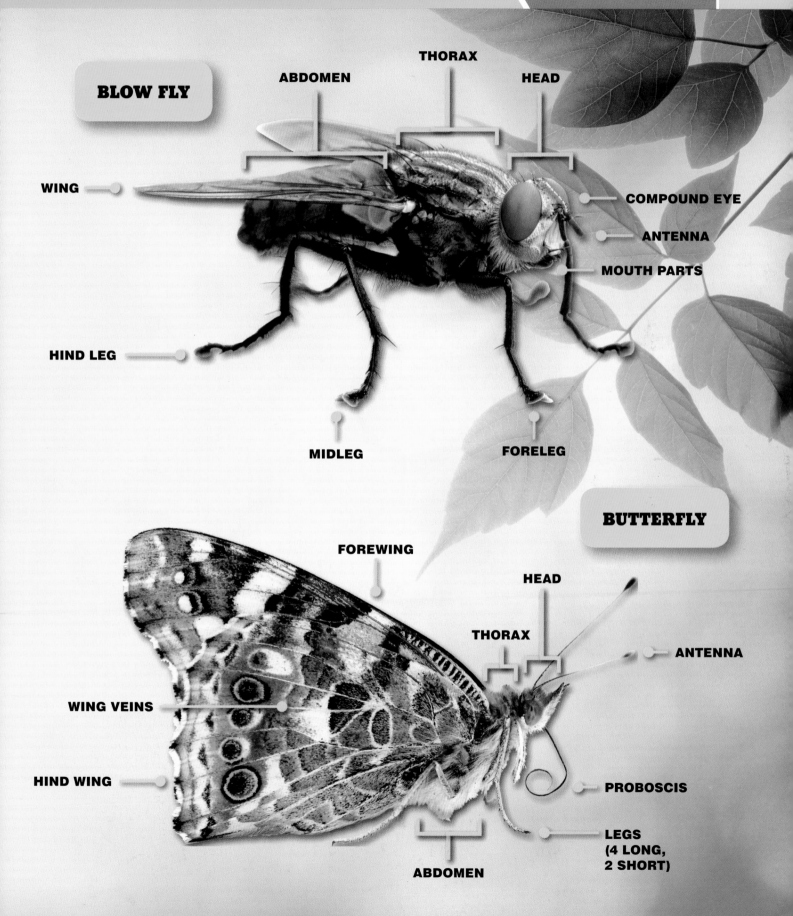

BLOW FLY

ABDOMEN

THORAX

HEAD

WING

COMPOUND EYE

ANTENNA

MOUTH PARTS

HIND LEG

MIDLEG

FORELEG

BUTTERFLY

FOREWING

HEAD

THORAX

ANTENNA

WING VEINS

HIND WING

PROBOSCIS

LEGS
(4 LONG,
2 SHORT)

ABDOMEN

HRABE'S JUMPING BRISTLETAIL

Scientific name: *Machilis hrabei*
Pronunciation: *MAK-ih-lis hray-BAY-ee*
Body length: 1/2 inch
Food: Lichens and mosses
Habitat: Leaf litter, under stones, moist soil
Distribution: Global

FAST FACT They may not have wings, but that doesn't mean they're stuck on the ground. A jumping bristletail can pop into the air as much as 12 inches by arching its body and then slamming its abdomen into the ground.

NON-WINGED HEXAPOD ORDERS

TOTAL SPECIES:
10,765

Protura
(pruh-TYUR-uh)
➡ Proturans
804 species

Collembola
(kuh-LEM-buh-luh)
➡ Springtails
8,130 species

Diplura
(duh-PLUR-uh)
➡ Two-pronged
bristletails
800 species

Archaeognatha
(ar-kee-og-NAY-thuh)
➡ Jumping bristletails
504 species

Zygentoma
(zye-gen-TOH-muh)
➡ Silverfish
527 species

Non-Winged Hexapods

AT A GLANCE

Small, tough non-winged hexapods are some of the oldest animals in the world. They include three orders that are insect cousins but not actually insects: Protura, Collembola, and Diplura. For more than 450 million years, most of these animals have existed relatively unchanged amid a changing world.

A hexapod is an animal with six legs. The animals in this section have six legs. They also do not have wings.

➡ Proturans are so small, they cannot be identified without a microscope.

➡ Proturans add segments to their bodies as they molt.

➡ Diplura can regrow their rear leglike organs— called "cerci"—if they are broken off by a predator or by accident.

➡ Silverfish are, obviously, not fish, but their wiggling movements can look like those of a swimming fish.

Springtails are small, but they're hardy. They live on every continent. Moist soil is their favorite habitat, but they are also found in dry places such as deserts, or rocky areas, as long as there is some decaying plant matter around to eat. They are active at night. Their hard outer shells help them survive. They are among the few insects that keep molting (replacing an outer shell) as adults. They become a little bit bigger after each molt—that's the springtail growth process. So the young look just like the adults, only smaller.

FLIP AND FLY

A springtail has a way to "get air" without flying. A body part called a furca is attached to a segment of the body. It folds under the abdomen. When the springtail pushes the furca out from under the abdomen, it lifts the insect off the ground as high as 7 inches.

BODY TYPES

Springtails generally have one of three body types. The ones that live mostly underground come in very plain colors and have stout body shapes.

Others are more like colorful little blobs, called globular (from "globe"). And the springtail body type seen in some of the largest species, such as the one in this picture, is more elongated with larger antennae.

JUMPING BRISTLETAIL GALLERY

Some scientists think that these wingless creatures may not actually be insects, but they are all non-winged hexapods.

BANKSI BRISTLETAIL

Scientific name: *Machiloides banksi*
Body length: 1/4 inch
Food: Plant matter
Habitat: Under rocks, moist soil
Distribution: Southern and eastern United States

FAST FACT Many jumping bristletails have huge compound eyes. Instead of two pupils, they can have hundreds or thousands of pupil-like eye parts.

JUMPING JACK

Scientific name: *Petrobius maritimus*
Body length: 3/4 inch
Food: Algae
Habitat: Tidal basin
Distribution: Edges of Mediterranean and North Seas

FAST FACT They have weaker mouthparts than others in this group, but that's not a problem since their diet is soft and squishy algae.

GERMAN ROCKHOPPER

Scientific name: *Lepismachilis y-signata*
Body length: 1/2 inch
Habitat: Under stone, quarry, leaf litter
Food: Algae, lichen
Distribution: Europe

FAST FACT Scientists are studying the way these insects take in olfactory (smell) information, which is different from how most insects do. This is no wonder, considering that jumping bristletails are considered the most primitive order of true insects.

Silverfish: Homebodies

Most people have seen quick-moving silverfish scuttling around their homes. Silverfish live in the wild, too, but they find many things to eat where people live. Silverfish eat the paste out of books, so they can often be found in libraries. Why paste? They like sugar, whether in the form of starch in book bindings or in a kitchen pantry. Silverfish like to live in cool, damp places, so they may make their homes under furniture or appliances. They also like the dark, so that's why they scurry away when people flip on a light switch.

MATING HABITS

To mate, a silverfish male deposits his sperm in little packets on and around plants. A female then picks them up and mixes them with her eggs. Once the eggs are fertilized, the female lays them to be hatched.

BUG BEHAVIOR

Homeowners can put up with a few silverfish. But if this insect shows up in large numbers, it can do a lot of damage. Silverfish eat the paste that holds up wallpaper, for instance. If they eat enough of the paste, the wallpaper can be damaged or even fall down.

NAME GAME

Silverfish get their name from the metallic sheen of their fishlike scales.

Fish scales

Silverfish scales

SILVERFISH GALLERY

They are not very silver, and they are not fish. But keep an eye out in kitchens and bathrooms for these creatures "swimming" across the floor.

URBAN SILVERFISH

Scientific name: *Ctenolepisma urbana*
Body length: Up to 3/4 inch
Food: Starchy products, often found in homes
Habitat: Building interior
Distribution: Global

FAST FACT Also known as the giant silverfish, this species is often found in cities and large buildings.

FOUR-LINED SILVERFISH

Scientific name: *Ctenolepisma lineata*
Body length: 1/2 inch
Food: Starchy products found in homes
Habitat: Building interior
Distribution: Eastern and midwestern United States

FAST FACT This type of silverfish is often found in wooden-roofed structures.

FIREBRAT

Scientific name:
Thermobia domestica
Body length: 1/2 inch
Food: Human food waste
Habitat: Warm building interior
Distribution: Global

FAST FACT This type of silverfish prefers a warmer environment, so it is often found living beneath stoves or furnaces.

Collembola come in a variety of colors, shapes, and sizes.

Springtail

Bear-bodied springtail

Globular springtail

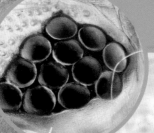

Silverfish have compound eyes.

Globular springtail

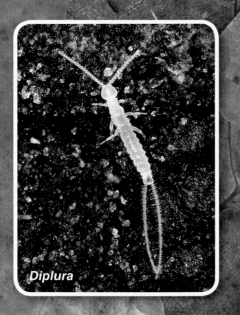

Diplura

Macro portrait of a springtail, showing extreme detail.

Elongated-body springtail

CONEHEADS

Proturans are primitive hexapods. They are less than a tenth of an inch long. They are very primitive animals, lacking eyes and antennae. They grow a new body segment with each molt, reaching an adult length of 12 abdominal segments.

Globular springtail

Making Change...Simply

Some insects go through simple metamorphosis. That means basically that they don't change body types; they just get bigger as they age. Many of them add wings during this process, too. Insects that go through simple metamorphosis include dragonflies, grasshoppers, cockroaches, termites, and true bugs. Simple metamorphosis has three stages.

STAGE ONE: EGG

A male insect fertilizes the eggs carried by a female insect. The female then lays one egg at a time (like some bedbugs) or tens of thousands (like some moths). After the eggs are laid, nearly all insects leave their eggs behind to survive on their own. One exception is shield bugs, some species of which guard their eggs until they hatch. The photo at right shows stink bug eggs beginning to hatch.

STAGE TWO: NYMPH

After eggs hatch, a young insect undergoing simple metamorphosis usually looks like a mini-version of the adult. For example, a very young termite looks essentially like an adult termite. This young insect is called a nymph. If it is born and lives in the water, it is called a naiad. The photo below shows a stink bug nymph.

STAGE THREE: ADULT

In the process of becoming an adult, the insect sheds its skin over and over. This is called molting. Each time it molts, it has grown a bit more. Some insects molt just a few times, while others molt dozens of times. Eventually the insect is an adult, and molting stops. However, all non-winged hexapods continue to molt through adulthood, and protura are unique in adding body segments as they molt through immature stages.

Nearly all insects begin in the same way. The adult female lays eggs—either one at a time or in large batches, depending on the species. Some eggs are laid in water, others in soil, still others on the leaves of plants. Some eggs are deposited inside plants...or even inside other animals. After the eggs hatch, insects go through either simple or complete metamorphosis to become adults.

MACRO

Insect eggs come in many shapes and sizes. This image shows some of the extremes that can occur even within one group of insects. The larger egg is 1/10 of an inch across and comes from *Haaniella echinata*, a stick insect from Borneo. The very tiny egg is from another stick insect, of the genus *Micadina*.

WATER BORN

Some insects lay eggs in water, including the female emperor dragonfly shown here.

BEFORE AND AFTER

When an insect molts, it sheds its old exoskeleton, leaving behind an empty replica of itself.

Cockroach

Leafhopper

Mantis

A Complete Makeover

The other type of insect development is called complete metamorphosis. In this way of growing, there is a fourth step in the process, and young insects look completely different from the adults. Insects that go through complete metamorphosis include butterflies, moths, bees, ants, flies, and wasps. Complete metamorphosis has four stages.

STAGE ONE: EGG

All insects that undergo complete metamorphosis start out as eggs. The eggs can be tiny or large, alone or part of a cluster. Social species of bee are one group that lays large batches of eggs; adult bees build small cells inside their hives for each egg. The photo shows monarch butterfly eggs.

STAGE FOUR: ADULT

After forming for days, weeks, or longer in its little sac, the adult insect emerges. It looks very different from the larva. The adult often has wings, longer antennae, and longer, different legs. It also now has the ability to reproduce.

STAGE TWO: LARVA

A young insect is called a larva once it emerges from the egg. Different insects have different kinds of larvae (the plural of larva), including caterpillars for butterflies and moths, and grubs for some beetles. The photo shows a monarch butterfly larva.

STAGE THREE: PUPA

The larva's job is to eat and grow until it is ready to change. For this stage, it creates a sac called a pupa. Inside this pupa, the insect goes through amazing changes—the complete metamorphosis. For example, a squishy caterpillar transforms into a beautiful, colorful, winged butterfly.

LARVAL LOOKS

Insect larvae comes in many shapes and sizes, depending on the species.

Rhinoceros beetle grub (larva)

Mosquito larvae in water

Ladybug pupae on grass

GROWTH SPURTS

Ants grow from egg to larva to pupa as they undergo complete metamorphosis. These photos show, from top to bottom, the transformation from larva to pupa.

GIANT MAYFLY

Scientific name: *Hexagenia limbata*
Pronunciation: *heks-uh-JEEN-ee-uh lim-BAH-tuh*
Wingspan: 1–1-1/2 inches
Food: Algae and plant matter (nymph stage only)
Habitat: Pond, river, stream
Distribution: Northern North America

FAST FACT The giant mayfly is one of the largest of the ephemeroptera order, and the females can weigh up to twice as much as the males of the species.

PRIMITIVE-WINGED INSECTS ORDERS

TOTAL SPECIES:
8,726

Ephemeroptera
(uh-fem-uh-ROP-tuh-ruh)
➡ Mayflies
3,046 species

Odonata
(oh-duh-NAH-tuh)
➡ Dragonflies
and damselflies
5,680 species

Primitive-Winged Insects

AT A GLANCE

The wings of the insects in this group can't be folded over their abdomens, which sets them apart from all other winged insects. Because they never evolved this ability, they are called primitive-winged insects.

➡ Primitive-winged insects have four wings that can move independently.

➡ Fossil evidence shows mayflies existed 350 million years ago.

➡ Most mayflies are less than 1 inch long.

➡ The ancestors of dragonflies first lived more than 300 million years ago.

➡ Some early insects that were relatives of today's dragonflies had wings that were more than 2 feet across.

➡ Dragonflies are among the largest flying insects, with bodies as long as 5 inches.

➡ Damselflies are smaller than dragonflies but have similar long, thin body shapes and wide wingspans.

The scientific name of this order includes a clue to its most famous feature. *Ephemero* means "having a short life," which describes most mayfly species. Adult mayflies may live for a few minutes or slightly more than a day. But they are actually alive much longer than that. After hatching from eggs, young mayflies live in water using gills to breathe, where they eat and grow for as long as four years.

These young mayflies are known as naiads because they live in the water. Naiads undergo a simple metamorphosis. While emerging from the water, a mayfly expands its body and cracks open an outer shell. In this phase, the mayfly is known as a subimago. It emerges with wings, ready to fly in just minutes.

Most mayflies then go through another change to become full adults. Mayflies are the only living group of insects that undergo molting in a winged form. The adult mayfly mates and then dies, usually within 24 hours. Adult mayflies don't even have mouths for eating.

WORD

A **naiad** *(NEYE-ad)* is a baby insect that lives in water. In Greek mythology, the Naiads (also known as nymphs) were minor gods who lived near water; they protected young women.

SWARMING MAYFLIES

Mayflies usually emerge from the water between late spring and early fall. In 2014, a massive swarm of mayflies poured out of the Mississippi River from Davenport, Iowa, through St. Paul, Minnesota. The vast hordes of insects created clouds that were spotted by satellites in space. The insects covered buildings and streets. Within days, the piles of dead mayflies were so big that snowplows were needed to clean up.

Mayfly naiad

MAYFLY GALLERY

If you see these insects in the wild, enjoy it while it lasts and try to snap a picture. Most won't live more than a few days.

EASTERN GREEN DRAKE

Scientific name: *Ephemera guttulata*
Body length: 3/4–1 inch
Food: Nymphs eat plant matter; adults don't eat.
Habitat: Shallow lake and bay, slow-moving river
Distribution: Eastern and southern United States

FAST FACT Green drakes are a swarming species of mayfly. Their dead bodies can create piles that are several feet deep.

BLUE-WINGED OLIVE

Scientific name: *Baetis tricaudatus*
Body length: 3/4 inch
Food: Nymphs eat plant matter; adults don't eat.
Habitat: River, stream, pond
Distribution: North America

FAST FACT Fishermen going after river trout make lures designed to look like these insects, which are the favorite food of many species of trout.

SAND MINNOW

Scientific name: *Ametropus ammophilus*
Body length: 1/2–1 inch
Food: Nymphs eat plant matter; adults don't eat.
Habitat: Large river
Distribution: Northwestern United States

FAST FACT The common name of this species comes from the sandy area where it lives.

Dragonflies and their relatives the damselflies make up the order Odonata. *Odon* means "tooth." These insects don't have teeth, but they do have sharp mouthparts. They use the mouthparts to crush up insects, which are their main food. Dragonflies have four wings that stick out from their bodies. Each wing can move on its own, enabling these insects to fly backward or forward. Huge compound eyes allow dragonflies to see in almost every direction, which helps in tracking down flying prey. A dragonfly can snag insects with its legs and carry them away to eat.

GET OUT OF MY HOUSE

Dragonflies are territorial. That means they defend their turf from other dragonflies that want to hunt there. The males are especially fierce and will chase any rival that nears their area.

BUG BEHAVIOR

When dragonflies eat, they eat well. Some can consume hundreds of mosquitoes in one day. Dragonflies can hunt only when flying. If a dragonfly cannot fly because of an injury, it will starve to death.

BUILT-IN SHADES The compound eyes of a dragonfly are not prone to sun glare, allowing them to easily navigate over water.

Damselflies live most of their lives as naiads underwater, emerging as adults. They have four wide wings like dragonflies do. When resting, though, damselflies fold their wings back a bit, while dragonflies keep them fully extended. Damselflies are also generally smaller and have more slender bodies. They skim over and near water to search for prey. They perch and then dart out when they see suitable prey instead of flying constantly.

Damselfly

Dragonfly

HOLD IT!

Damselflies and dragonflies can't rest without holding on to something, but it works out, because they can perch on almost anything.

Flat surface?
No problem.

A flower bud provides numerous footholds.

The damselfly lives most of its life as a naiad underwater. It breathes through small gills on its tail. These gills drop away with the exoskeleton when the insect emerges to become a flying adult.

BRENDAN SAYS

Odonate naiads are fierce underwater predators and can grab and eat small vertebrates, including fish. They are able to thrust out their jaws with lightning speed and clamp on to other animals with a death grip.

The tiniest stick works for this damselfly

Even a flower petal makes for a perch

A steady hand will do in a pinch

Wide-winged and long-bodied, dragonflies and damselflies are some of the fastest insects in the world. They speed through the air over ponds and streams.

GIANT DARNER

Scientific name: *Anax walsinghami*
Body length: 4–5-1/2 inches inches
Habitat: Pond, slow-flowing
  river and stream
Food: Insects
Distribution: Southwestern
  North America

FAST FACT With a wingspan that can reach more than 5 inches, the giant darner is the largest dragonfly species in North America.

COMMON GREEN DARNER

Scientific name: *Anax junius*
Body length: 2-1/2–3 inches
Habitat: Pond, marsh
Food: Insects
Distribution: North America

FAST FACT Researchers placed tiny transmitters on some common green darners and then tracked them using satellites. They found that the insects could cover about 7.5 miles per day.

WANDERING GLIDER

Scientific name: *Pantala flavescens*
Body length: 1-3/4 inches
Habitat: Pool and pond, often created by rain
Food: Insects
Distribution: Global, except for Europe and Antarctica

FAST FACT Scientists have traced the migration of this aptly named insect 11,000 miles across the Indian Ocean, the longest known distance traveled by any insect. Wandering gliders have also been spotted in the Himalaya mountain range, 24,000 feet above sea level—the greatest recorded height achieved by a dragonfly.

WESTERN FLYING ADDER

Scientific name:
 Cordulegaster dorsalis
Body length: 3 inches
Habitat:
 Woods, near stream
Food: Insects
Distribution:
 Western North America

FAST FACT This adder is a dragonfly that hunts near the surface of water.

NORTHERN BLUET

Scientific name:
 Enallagma cyathigerum
Body length:
 1–1-1/2 inches
Habitat: Pond,
 marshy lake shore
Food: Insects
Distribution: Europe

FAST FACT Because most bluets live in climates with cold winters, the naiads of this species can live under ice.

TWELVE-SPOTTED SKIMMER

Scientific name:
 Libellula pulchella
Body length:
 1-3/4—2-1/4 inch
Habitat: Pond,
 slow-moving stream
Food: Insects
Distribution: United States, southern Canada

FAST FACT
The twelve-spotted skimmer has a colorful body shorter in length than its large wingspan.

Eastern pondhawks are green at birth. The male develops a blue body at maturity.

Some dragonflies—like the Kirby's dropwing—use a handstand-like position, or obelisk posture, to prevent overheating.

Halloween pennant

Blue-fronted dancer

Pied paddy skimmer

Mayfly eyes look like speakers.

Bluet damselfly

Southern darters extend their wings forward to regulate body temperature.

Blue dasher

The migrant hawker's long body has ten brightly-colored abdominal segments.

DID YOU KNOW?

In China, dragonflies are associated with success and harmony and are considered to be good-luck charms.

Red-eyed damselfly

The expression *bug-eyed* is perfect when someone makes their eyes look big and round. The term comes from the insect world, in which many insects boast enormous eyes that cover large parts of their heads. But those eyes are more than just big; they are some of the most interesting eyes in the animal kingdom.

SIMPLE EYES ON THE SIDE

Larvae of insects that go through complete metamorphosis have different kinds of simple eyes, called lateral ocelli. These ocelli are located on the side of the larva's head and also can can form images and, when clustered together, may function similarly to a compound eye. They are very small on the caterpillar shown here.

SIMPLE EYES ON TOP

Many insects that have compound eyes have another, smaller set of sight organs as well. Located on the top of the insect's head, they are called dorsal ocelli (*oh-SEH-lye*). They often look like tiny black bumps, as shown here. These ocelli can sense only light and dark. Bees, wasps, and dragonflies are examples of insects that have these "bonus" eyes.

WORD

The word **dorsal** is used to describe something that is on top of an animal's body, such as dorsal ocelli, or a dorsal fin on a fish.

Insects have the same senses that humans do: sight, taste, touch, hearing, and smell. And some can sense other kinds of light, or even magnetic fields. But their bodies take in sense information in different and fantastic ways.

MACRO

This close-up of the compound eye of a fly shows how the dome of the eye is made up of hundreds of tiny organs.

COMPOUND EYES

Instead of having one pupil per eye as most animals do, many insects have compound eyes with multiple organs of sight. (*Compound* means something is made up of many smaller, similar parts.) Each eye is packed with thousands of microscopic organs that gather in light. Cool science word alert: Those individual organs are called ommatidia (*ah-muh-TID-ee-uh*). Dragonflies have as many as 28,000 of them in each compound eye. Scientists are not sure how these eyes work. Does an insect see a whole picture with each part of its eye? Or does its brain gather the many parts into one picture? Or does the picture look like a mosaic? Scientists are still looking for the answers to these questions.

Touch, Smell, and Taste

Insects have interesting eyes, but their sight is generally the least dominant of their senses. Touch, smell, and taste give most insects a lot more information than they get from vision.

BRISTLY SHELLS

Insects do not have the same kind of skin as most animals. Instead, most adults have hard exoskeletons that are both skeleton and skin. The exoskelton is full of nerve endings, even at the base of bristles all over their bodies. Their bristles are much more important in feeling out the world around them, though.

WORD

Chemoreceptors react to chemicals or smells in the air. An insect with these organs uses them like other animals might use their nose.

SUPER SENSES

Some insects use their senses in particularly interesting ways:

The snout moth is one of many insects that has small mouthpart organs called palps on its face to taste food sources before eating.

An ant nest beetle can sense the chemical trail of ants with its antennae. It can then follow that trail to its food source.

Butterflies and blow flies are among the insects that have chemoreceptors in their feet that help them "taste" potential food.

TUNING IN

Nearly all insects have antennae at some stage of their lives. The antennae are covered in sensitive hairs that can feel physical objects, sense chemicals in the air, and detect movement nearby. In some ways, antennae are more like noses that take in information than fingers that touch. Cave crickets have extremely long antennae to help them in their dark environment. Mosquitoes can use their antennae to feel the wingbeats of possible female mates.

Paper wasp

Longhorn beetle

Gypsy Moth

The compound eyes of some flies add another layer of sense: Tiny hairs stick out between the individual eye organs, combining sight and touch.

Mosquitoes can smell the carbon dioxide that animals exhale. They use that to locate prey. But they can also detect your body heat to track you down.

Scientists think that the iron in a bee's body helps it navigate using Earth's magnetic field.

Listen Up

How do insects sense the sounds that their species and the world make? Most hear by detecting vibrations from sound waves in the air, just as humans and many other animals do. However, hearing happens in different parts of an insect's body. Katydids, for example, have small patches on their legs through which they hear. And some insects, including mosquitoes and bees, hear through small patches of skin and nerve cells on the antennae called Johnston's organs. This organ takes in sound waves and sends them to the insect's brain to decipher.

MACRO

The small tympanum patches on the legs of crickets and katydids are their "ears." The patches are made of skin that vibrates in the presence of sound. In a human, the tympanum, called an eardrum, is located in the middle ear.

ON THE FLY

Crickets and cicadas are well-known noisemakers. But what about ants? In 2013, British researchers recorded *Myrmica scabrinodis* pupae making a scratching sound. After investigating, they found that the developing ants were rubbing spikes on their legs against their abdomens. The scratching sound was a signal to other ants in the colony.

A CHORUS OF INSECTS

Here are some of the other sounds of the world's insect orchestra.

Cicadas thrum
A body part called a tymbal vibrates like a drum on the abdomen of the cicada. The rapidly moving tymbal creates a *hmmmmmm* sound.

Death's head moths squeak
If this moth does not like what is happening, it vibrates a part of its mouth to make a short, sharp *eeeeee* sound.

Bees buzz
Flapping their wings more than 400 times per second, bees create a very familiar *bzzzzzz* sound.

Cockroaches hiss
These insects can force air through breathing holes in their sides to create a *ssssss* sound.

INSECT SOUNDS

Crickets are among the best known noisemaking insects. They rub their wings together to make a chirping sound. The rubbing movement is called stridulation. The pattern and tone of the chirps is different from species to species. For example, a field cricket sounds different from a house cricket. Some beetles stridulate, as well. European ground beetles, some dung beetles, the horned passalus, and the aptly named click beetles will make clicking sounds when disturbed. And if you pick up a june bug, expect to hear some buzzing as it struggles.

At some point in their lives, most insect species can fly, and many can fly very quickly. They beat their wings very rapidly to take off. Here are some fast fliers from the insect world.

House fly
House flies can beat their wings up to 200 times per second. That's more than twice as fast as a hummingbird.

Butterfly in flight
With more than 15,000 species, butterfly speeds vary greatly, but most fly from 5 to 12 mph. To generate speed, they can rotate their wings, getting power from both the up and down motions.

Bald-faced hornet
Hornets can fly more than 21 mph. This bald-faced hornet is aggressive, and can sting multiple times when threatened.

HOPPERS
Grasshoppers and crickets can fly, but they usually don't need to. Their large hind legs give them enormous power for hopping great distances.

They fly, they walk, they hop, they crawl, they skitter. Insects use a wide variety of ways to move around their environments. Each helps a particular insect thrive in its habitat.

DRAGONFLIES

These insects are among the best fliers. Their four wings can operate independently. That is, each can beat or turn on its own instead of flapping in the same way and at the same time as the others.

HUMMINGFLIES?

One of the best insect fliers is the hoverfly. Hoverfly species can fly very quickly in any direction, and they also have the ability to hold themselves in the air in one place. And hawk moths are sometimes called hummingbird moths because of the similarity of their flight and hover patterns to those of hummingbirds.

Hawk moth

Many insects move mostly on the ground, even if they can fly. Using their six legs, they can walk, run, or jump. If you observe, for instance, a quick-moving beetle, it might seem as if those many legs would get tangled up—but a system of movement has evolved to make it all work out.

SWIMMING BEETLES

Insects don't just move on land. They get wet, too.

Diving beetles use large pads on their front legs like paddles, pulling themselves through the water as they dive into ponds in search of prey.

Naiads of some dragonflies scoot around underwater using a propulsion system of sorts—water pushed backward out of their bodies moves the juvenile insects forward.

Water striders are light enough to walk on the surface of water; specialized hairs on their feet help distribute their weight so they don't sink.

Insect walking

TRIPOD GAIT

When a six-legged insect walks, it has only three legs on the ground with each step. Those three provide support while the other three legs are used for stepping forward. This is called a tripod gait: one leg touches the ground on one side of the body, and two legs touch on the other; with each step, that arrangement of feet on the ground switches from side to side. When it changes speed, its leg pattern switches to suit its gait. If it creeps slowly, it may only lift one leg at a time, and if it runs at high speeds, it may alternate on only its two hind legs, like a cockroach.

WALK THIS WAY

Caterpillars, the larvae of butterflies and moths, often have two kinds of legs. They have six called true legs, and they also have leglike parts called prolegs that provide additional support. They can walk using many legs at once. Their large bodies also help them move forward by undulating (moving like a wave).

Prolegs

True legs

DID YOU KNOW?

Tree-dwelling ants can walk upside down. They have hooked claws at the ends of their feet to help them hold on.

ON THE FLY

Researchers in California claim that the cheetah is no longer the fastest animal. Using high-speed video, they determined that a type of mite is the fastest—sort of. Instead of measuring speed in miles per hour, they calculated how fast the mite moved in body lengths per second. Using that measure, the mite runs 20 times faster than a cheetah.

Water strider

ORTHOPTEROIDS ORDERS

TOTAL SPECIES:

42,277

Plecoptera
(pluh-KOP-tuh-ruh)
➡ Stoneflies
3,497 species

Embiodea
(em-bee-OH-dee-uh)
➡ Webspinners
458 species

Phasmatodea
(faz-muh-TOH-dee-uh)
➡ Stick insects
2,853 species

Orthoptera
(or-THOP-tuh-ruh)
➡ Crickets, grasshoppers, and katydids
23,616 species

Dermaptera
(dur-MAP-tuh-ruh)
➡ Earwigs
1,967 species

Notoptera
(noh-TOP-tuh-ruh)
➡ *Gladiators and ice crawlers*
39 species

Isoptera
(i-SOP-tuh-ruh)
➡ Termites
2,864 species

Blattaria
(bluh-TAIR-ee-uh)
➡ Cockroaches
4,565 species

Mantodea
(man-TOH-dee-uh)
➡ Mantises
2,384 species

Zoraptera
(zuh-RAP-tuh-ruh)
➡ Zorapterans
34 species

MALAYSIAN ORCHID MANTIS

Scientific name: *Hymenopus coronatus*
Pronunciation: *hye-men-OP-us kor-uh-NOT-us*
Body length: 2-1/2–3 inches
Habitat: Rain forest
Food: Other insects, anything it can catch
Distribution: Southeast Asia

FAST FACT This insect hides among the flowers of its rain forest home. When prey comes by, it uses its lightning-quick front legs to snatch it up.

Can you spot the Malaysian orchid mantis?

Orthopteroids

AT A GLANCE

If you look at a grasshopper, a termite, and a cockroach side by side, it is not obvious why they are all orthopteroids. The answer is in the wings. Most of the insects in this superorder have small wing parts called tegmina. The Greek word *orthos* means "straight"; the tegmina in these animals are stiff, straight, and hard.

➡ Orthopteroids all have chewing mouthparts.

➡ Cockroaches have been around for more than 350 million years.

➡ Though they spend most of their time walking, most of the adults can fly at some point in their life cycles.

➡ Many orthopteroids can make and hear sounds. Some of these sounds are out of the range of what can be detected by human ears.

Termites are famous for one thing—eating wood. A colony can include anywhere from hundreds to millions of termites. Buildings are often made of wood, so termites can do a lot of damage to places where people live and work. This gives termites a bad reputation, but this behavior also helps the ecosystem by breaking down rotten wood, which makes good soil for the growth of forests, meadows, and grasslands. This termite activity lets water seep into the ground, creating better conditions for fertile soil to form.

HELP WANTED

A termite is born to carry out one of a small number of jobs. It has a particular task from birth, and this task never changes. The list of jobs varies a bit from species to species, but it may include the following roles:

Queen: Lays millions of eggs, one at a time (sometimes as fast as an egg per second); her egg-laying abdomen is more than ten times larger than her head

King: Fertilizes all the eggs

Reproductives: Smaller winged termites that can also reproduce; swarm out to start new nests every few years; also known as alates

Workers: Build the nest

Soldiers: Protect the nest; some species protect the colony by spraying nasty-smelling goo at attackers

NESTING PLACE

Termites that live underground in Africa and Australia (where they are known as "white ants") build some of the most enormous nests in the animal kingdom. A termite system of caves, tunnels, and chambers can cover several acres underground. Termites build cones of dirt more than 20 feet tall above the main entrances to their nests. Tubes in the cones let the hot underground air escape. More than 5 million termites can live in the largest nests.

TERMITES GALLERY

If you live in a wooden house or building, you may be living with termites. If there are enough of them, they can cause real damage.

FUNGUS-GROWING TERMITES

Scientific name:
Macrotermitinae (subfamily)
Body length: 1/2 inch
Habitat: Wood structure, underground nest
Food: Wood, fungus
Distribution: Africa, Australia

FAST FACT Termites from this subfamily are a source of protein for many people in Africa. The larger insects are fried and eaten, and large amounts of them can be used to create cooking oil.

FORMOSAN SUBTERRANEAN TERMITE

Scientific name: *Coptotermes formosanus*
Body length: 1/2 inch
Habitat: Wood structure, underground nest
Food: Wood
Distribution: Asia, southern United States

FAST FACT This species came to north America from East Asia. The size of its underground colonies, which are comprised of millions of individuals, means it can cause extensive damage quickly.

DAMPWOOD TERMITES

Scientific name: *Termopsidae* (family)
Body length: 1/2–1 inch
Habitat: Rotten wood
Food: Wood
Distribution: Global, above and below equator

FAST FACT Because dampwood termites prefer moist wood, they are not as destructive to houses as are drywood termites.

INSECTS AT WORK

Subterranean termites live in the soil, where they may get into the foundation of a house—the part built underground. Signs of an infestation may include swarming, mud tubes, and wood damage.

When people think of hated insects, cockroaches probably come to mind. They are among the most widespread species of insects, and they can eat just about anything. Cockroaches can hide in the tiniest of spaces—some can squeeze into spaces as thin as a quarter. Cockroaches have been around for more than 350 million years, and experts think they can survive nearly anything.

4
3
2
1
0

LIFE SIZE

The Central American giant cockroach is considered the world's longest. Found in Central America and northern South America, this sizable critter can be found in rainforest habitats. It is huge, at nearly 4 inches long.

Cockroaches can actually live for quite a while without their heads. They breathe through organs on their sides. Their other organs are in their abdomens and thoraces, and the nerves controlling them are spread throughout their bodies, not just in their heads. Headless roaches eventually die from dehydration, since they have no way to drink.

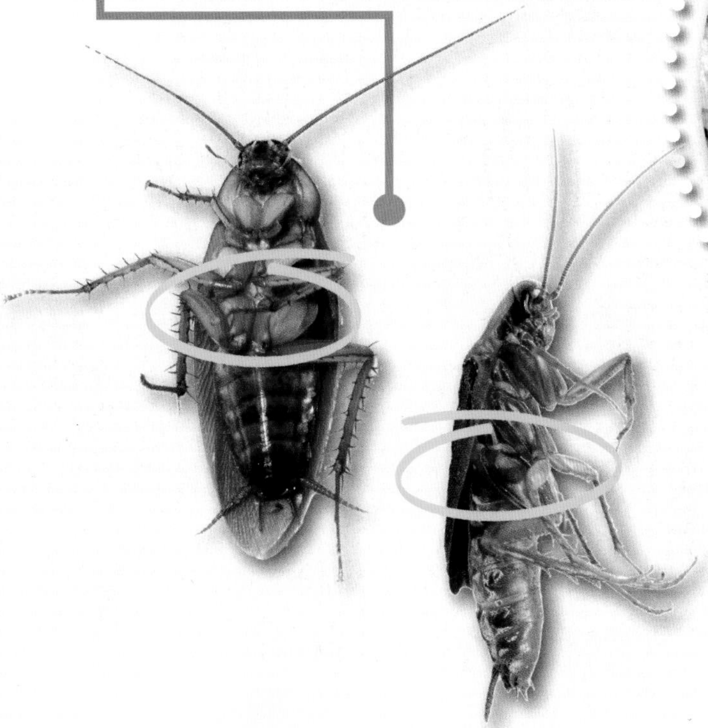

PORTABLE EGGS

Female cockroaches can lay more than 200 eggs a year. Most species keep the eggs in special sacs called oothecae (*oh-uh-THEE-kee*) until they hatch. Some carry their sacs with them, as shown above, while others find safe places to store them.

BRENDAN SAYS

Although cockroaches are best known as human pests, there are many species that live their entire lives outdoors and are important parts of thriving ecosystems. As scavengers, they eat decaying plant and animal tissue and help recycle nutrients. They also serve as food sources for other animals. Additionally, they are important to entomologists like me because in college we often learn how to dissect insects by first using cockroaches.

WORD

To **dissect** is to cut into a dead specimen of an animal in order to study it.

Cockroaches are survivors, with traits like hissing and spewing foul-smells to keep predators away.

MADAGASCAR GIANT HISSING COCKROACH

Scientific name: *Gromphadorhina portentosa*
Body length: 2–3 inches
Habitat: Forest floor, log
Food: Decaying plant or animal matter
Distribution: Madagascar

FAST FACT Yes, they hiss. These massive insects exhale through holes in their body, producing loud hissing sounds. These are often used as warnings to other cockroaches.

GERMAN COCKROACH

Scientific name: *Blatella germanica*
Body length: 1/2 inch
Habitat: Indoors
Food: Decaying plant or animal matter
Distribution: Global

FAST FACT These insects can climb walls, as their feet have thousands of tiny, bristly pads on the ends. The pads act like miniature suction cups. The German cockroach is one of the cockroaches most often found living among human beings.

GIANT BURROWING COCKROACH

Scientific name:
Macropanesthia rhinoceros
Body length: 3 inches
Habitat: Forest floor, often underground
Food: Decaying plant or animal matter
Distribution: Australia

FAST FACT At 1.2 ounces, this is the heaviest cockroach in the world. That's about the same as a slice of bread, or six U.S. quarters.

MARDI GRAS COCKROACH

Scientific name: *Polyzosteria mitchelli*
Body length: 2 inches
Habitat: Forest, grassland, meadow
Food: Decaying plant or animal matter
Distribution: Australia

FAST FACT If the colors don't scare off an attacker, the nasty smell this cockroach can spew should do the trick.

INSECTS AT WORK

Madagascar giant hissing cockroaches have become popular pets for people or classrooms looking for unusual animals. They are large and easy to see, don't seem to mind being handled, and look amazing.

There is more to this order of insects than the famous way that they appear to "pray." Long, thin, and hungry, mantises are some of the biggest eaters in the insect world. They have powerful jaws that can crack through insect exoskeletons. Their front legs have sharp spines used to snag and hold prey. Mantids look elegant and pretty, but bugs they're after should watch out. And not only bugs need to be on guard. Many species use camouflage so that they can remain motionless for a long time, waiting for prey to wander by. And mantids are unique among insects for their ability to turn their necks to look behind them.

NAME GAME

Why "praying"? The position of the praying mantis's front legs when it is resting make it resemble a person praying.

CRUNCH 'N' MUNCH

Mantids will eat anything they can capture. Here are some of their favorites.

Butterflies
Slow-flying butterflies are no match for fast-moving mantids.

Bees
Mantids wait by flowers and ambush bees as they approach.

EGG CASE

A female mantid puts her fertilized eggs into a sac called an ootheca. Then she leaves the sac behind after covering it with a thick, gooey substance that helps it stick to leaves or branches. The goo hardens to protect the eggs from predators until they hatch.

BUG BEHAVIOR

Yes, a praying mantis female does often eat her male while he mates with her. Many mantid species are cannibals—they eat their own kind, even their young.

Katydids
Even fellow orthopteroids become meals for hungry mantids.

Cicadas
A big cicada makes a tasty meal for a mantid.

Lizards
Even a small reptile like this lizard is within a mantid's grasp.

Masters of disguise as well as fierce predators, these insects lay in wait for prey to wander by.

MOSS MANTID

Scientific name: *Majangella moultoni*
Body length: 2–3 inches
Habitat: Rain forest
Food: Insects
Distribution: Southeast Asia

FAST FACT Not only does this mantid have green coloring so it can hide in moss, its body grows bumps and ridges that mimic the features of moss.

GIANT MALAYSIAN SHIELD MANTIS

Scientific name: *Rhombodera basalis*
Body length: 4–5 inches
Habitat: Rain forest
Food: Insects
Distribution: Southeast Asia

FAST FACT This blue-and-green mantis is one of the brightest mantids; it's also one of the largest species.

THISTLE MANTIS

Scientific name: *Blepharopsis mendica*
Body length: 2 inches
Habitat: Forest
Food: Insects
Distribution: Northern Africa

FAST FACT Mantids put on quite a show when threatened. They raise their front legs and spread their wings to look intimidating to predators.

INSECTS AT WORK

Praying mantises arrived in North America from Europe in 1899. They were brought in to kill gypsy moths, which were hurting farmers' crops. But the mantises were so busy eating one another that they didn't eat very many moths.

LEAF-LITTER MANTID

Scientific name: *Deroplatys trigonodera*
Body length: 3–6 inches
Habitat: Rain forest
Food: Insects
Distribution: Southeast Asia

FAST FACT The leaf-litter mantid's body mimics the colors and veins on a dead leaf, allowing it to blend in perfectly with its habitat.

While many cockroaches are dark brown, the giant cockroach is pale in color, with a dark spot over its head.

Hooded praying mantis

Desert cockroach

Slender-necked mantis

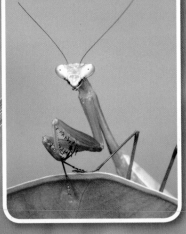

Worker termites

An adult reproductive termite has wings twice the size of its body.

The praying mantis has two large compound eyes, with three simple eyes between them.

Lichen bark mantis

The spiny flower mantis uses the eyespots on its forewings to scare away potential predators.

Taiwan flower mantis (green)

Wandering violin mantis

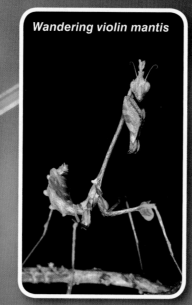

Ice crawlers live in cold climates, but when the temperature dips to 32 degrees Fahrenheit or below, they may freeze to death.

Ghost mantis

African Savannah mantid

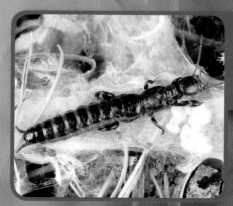

Web spinners spin silk tunnels and chambers for a damp and protective environment.

The ghost mantis comes in a variety of colors and is known as a miniature species, growing to about 2 inches long.

Chomp!

Insects don't have teeth, so they can't chew food the way people do. They have different ways of eating. Many insects use their mouths to bite and grab prey. The main mouthparts used by such insects are called mandibles. In most insects, these come together from each side, instead of from top and bottom as in humans and other mammals. Insects with chewing mouthparts usually eat food that requires chomping to break down plant parts or dead animals, or subdue live ones.

The titan beetle is one of the world's biggest insects and also the beetle with the longest body. It's no surprise that its mandibles are big and powerful enough to easily slice through skin. They have enough force to slice a pencil in half!

WORD

A **mandible** is a jawlike mouthpart in insects. Mandibles come in pairs, and each one works independently to open and close when the insect is eating.

NEARLY PERFECT

How does a dragonfly or damselfly catch prey in midair? Rather than chase its prey, it plots a path that will intercept, or cut off, the prey's flight. Dragonflies and damselflies are among the few animal groups that have this ability. One study found that they caught the prey they aimed at 97 percent of the time. Once the prey is caught, their strong jaws crunch and crunch until it is soft enough to swallow.

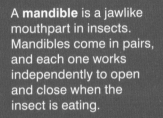

A dragonfly perches on a stem for its meal, after intercepting prey in the air and landing to eat that prey.

Like all animals, insects have to eat to survive. There is almost nothing in the world—flesh, plants, garbage, fungi, seeds, dung, and more—that is not food for one insect or another. To take in that food, each insect has its own way of eating that matches up best with what it eats: Some chomp, and others slurp.

CHEWING MOUTHPARTS

Grasshoppers, caterpillars, and beetles chomp through tough plant material before swallowing it.

Termites use their chewing mouthparts to bite into hard wood.

Cockroaches scavenge by chewing rotting matter and just about any other food they find along their way.

Predators like dragonflies and this mantis use mandibles to chomp their prey.

Slurp!

Not all insects bite into or chew their food—some slurp! These insects have long mouthparts that they use like straws to suck up their food. For some, such as butterflies, eating is as easy as finding a liquid food like plant or fruit juices. Bloodsucking insects have to work a little harder to find something to eat.

STAB AND SLURP

The assassin bug attacks quickly, grabbing its prey and stabbing it in the back with a sharp, pointed proboscis. Then it injects a type of saliva that dissolves the prey's insides. The resulting liquid can then be sucked up. What do assassin bugs eat? They prey on other small arthropods, chiefly insects.

MAC RO

A butterfly proboscis is shaped like a long, curly straw and stays rolled up until it's needed. It is shown here extended into a flower as the butterfly drinks nectar.

LIKE A SPONGE

To make sure its chosen meal can be slurped up, a fly will cover the food with saliva. This dissolves the food item into a mushy goo. The fly's mouthpart then works like a sponge, soaking up the liquid.

COMMON BLOODSUCKERS

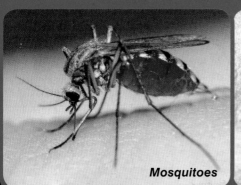

Mosquitoes

Bedbugs

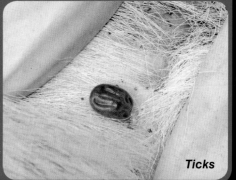

Ticks

Some insects spend their whole lives living close together with others of their kind. Ants and bees are the most well known social insects. These insects work as a group and will often move in swarms. Other swarms occur when large numbers of an insect species emerge at the same time or gather in large groups to mate.

SWARMING TO FOOD

When a scout ant locates a food source, it leaves a chemical trail. Quickly, hundreds or thousands of ants follow the trail to the food source (as shown in this photo). Each ant takes a part of it back to the colony to share.

LOOKING FOR A NEW NEIGHBORHOOD

Honeybees swarm with a specific purpose: to find a new home. Usually about once a year, a few scout bees will head out to locate a new place for the hive. When they return, the rest of the hive—including the queen—swarm to the new spot and begin building their new hive home.

With an estimated 10 quintillion insects living on Earth, it's not surprising that they often do so together. Many species live in huge gatherings, either in one place or on the move. When they move together as a large unit, it's called a swarm.

A CLOUD OF MAYFLIES

Mayflies are named for the time of year when they typically emerge, but it can happen in the summer as well, depending on the species, location, weather, and water temperature. In July 2014, a massive mayfly emergence from the Mississippi River was captured by National Weather Service radar.

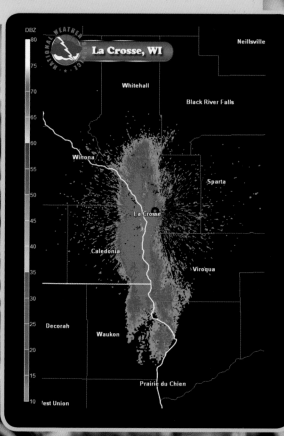

Locusts!

The most well-known type of swarming insect is the locust. For as long as people have been farming, they have feared massive swarms of these crop-destroying insects. Locusts affect 10 percent of the world's human population each year, and inhabit as much as 20 percent of the land's surface. The vast swarms emerge all at once and swarm in search of food.

▶ Madagascar, an island off the cost of eastern Africa, has been plagued with locusts. In 2013, locusts destroyed more than half the food crops on the island. One estimate said that more than 100 separate swarms buzzing around the island totaled more than 500 billion locusts. The locusts swarmed again in the spring of 2014.

GROUP NAMES

When locust swarms become large enough to damage crops, they are known as a "plague" of locusts. That comes from an Old Testament Bible story that told of a plague inflicted on the Egyptians by millions of locusts. Here are some other collective nouns for insect groups.

▶ **Army of ants**

▶ **Business of flies**

▶ **Flock of lice**

▶ **Loveliness of ladybugs**

HOME ON THE RANGE

Locusts once caused great destruction on the American Great Plains. In 1875, a swarm of Rocky Mountain locusts covered an area 1,800 by 110 miles. That made it by area the largest swarm of all time. Over time, due to farming of their breeding grounds, this type of locust has nearly disappeared from the United States.

STATS

According to a University of Florida report, a 1954 swarm of locusts in East Africa included a single-swarm, all-time record in terms of numbers of insects: 10 billion individual locusts. That's more than there are people on Earth.

► Scourge of mosquitoes

► Horde of gnats

► Kaleidoscope of butterflies

► Hive of bees

► Instrusion of cockroaches

The common name for stick insects comes from how they look: like sticks with legs. Walking sticks are long and thin. Their outer shells even take on the coloring or patterns of their leafy or woody homes. Walking sticks are able to blend in among trees, leaves, and branches. This camouflage helps keep them safe from predators. The insects wait patiently for darkness to start looking for food, which for them is mostly plant matter.

SOLO REPRODUCTION

Not all female walking sticks need males to reproduce. Many species use a process called parthenogenesis (*par-thuh-noh-JEN-uh-suhs*) to reproduce. That means the females don't need males to create new insects; eggs develop without fertilization. The females lay those eggs (shown here) on the ground by the dozens. At certain times, if enough females are present, the sound of the eggs hitting the ground can sound like rain.

LIFE SIZE

Get out your ruler. Most walking sticks are 4–6 inches in length, but some species can get really huge. The largest, Chan's megastick, is more than 22 inches long. The body of this giant walking stick—the largest in North America—is 7 inches long!

0   1   2   3   4   5   6   7

WALKING STICK GALLERY

Many insects in the walking stick family are long and thin and camouflage themselves on branches and twigs. Others like to stand out.

GREAT PHOBAETICUS

Scientific name: *Phobaeticus magnus*
Body length: 10–12 inches
Habitat: Forest, tree
Food: Plant matter
Distribution: Southeast Asia

FAST FACT The third-longest walking stick ever found, at more than 12.5 inches, was from this species.

CALIFORNIA TIMEMA

Scientific name: *Timema californica*
Body length: 1/2–1 inch
Habitat: Oak forest
Food: Plants
Distribution: West coast of North America

FAST FACT Timemas are cousins of walking sticks, but they disguise themselves among leaves. One that lives on a green leaf will be green, and one that lives among flowers more red in color. A timema can spew stinky stuff to warn off predators.

SPINY ACHRIOPTERA

Scientific name:
Achrioptera spinosissima
Body length: 10 inches
Habitat: Forest
Food: Plant matter
Distribution: Madagascar

FAST FACT Most stick insects are pretty drab looking. This species stands out for its amazing bright colors.

9   10   11   12

Grasshoppers, crickets, and katydids are all relatives. They have in common powerful back legs for jumping, and recognizable sounds, from the cricket's chirp to the grasshoppers' and katydids' "songs." They can form swarms when looking for food, and too many can devour a farmer's crops.

BRENDAN SAYS

Some of the loudest and most recognizable insect sounds come from Orthoptera. The sounds are specific to each species, so that individuals can recognize potential mates and also competitors for mates. The insects can recognize the pitches of the sounds, how long they last, and the spacing in between them.

INSECT ORCHESTRA

Male crickets and grasshoppers sing by rubbing parts of their legs or wings together very rapidly. This behavior attracts mates, warns rivals, or can claim a specific territory. The chirping sounds made by crickets differ from species to species; an expert can tell a cricket's species by how it chirps.

Crickets are nocturnal insects that get their name from the French word *criquer* (*kree-KAY*), which means to make a creaking sound. They are scavengers and omnivores, which means they eat both plant and animal matter that is already dead, instead of hunting for live prey.

TOO MANY!

During the Dust Bowl, a natural and manmade disaster in America in the 1930s, farmers had to contend with a decade-long drought and "storms" of dust that darkened the skies. They were also overrun with swarms of hungry grasshoppers that devastated the crops and whatever they could find in peoples' homes.

Though members of this group vary in body shape, size, and color, all have powerful rear legs, which many use for jumping.

JERUSALEM CRICKET

Scientific name: *Stenopelmatus fuscus*
Body length: 1–2 inches
Habitat: Under rock
Food: Plant matter, insects
Distribution: Western United States

FAST FACT The Jerusalem cricket's body is so heavy that it sometimes leaves a trail in the dust while walking. And it has to walk, because it does not have wings.

PAINTED GRASSHOPPER

Scientific name: *Dactylotum bicolor*
Body length: 3/4–1-3/8 inches
Habitat: Desert, light scrubland
Food: Plant matter
Distribution: Northern Mexico, southwestern and Great Plains United States

FAST FACT Most grasshoppers and crickets have very dull colors: greens, browns, and blacks. This multicolored species stands out, warning predators it is toxic.

DID YOU KNOW?

Crickets are considered good luck in many cultures, and they play a role in many Native American legends and stories.

LICHEN-COLORED KATYDID

Scientific name: *Markia hystrix*
Body length: 1-1/2–2 inches
Habitat: Forest with lichen
Food: Plant matter
Distribution: South America

FAST FACT Don't see it? Look again. This camouflage expert not only blends in with lichen on trees, it feeds on the same lichen. It grows spines and bumps that help it blend in.

COOLOOLA MONSTER

Scientific name: *Cooloola propator*
Body length: 1 inch
Habitat: Underground, desert areas
Food: Grubs
Distribution: Australia

FAST FACT These critters are somewhat like crickets, but they live underground and don't make noise. Their name comes from Cooloola Recreation Area in Great Sandy National Park, Queensland, where they live—and their scary appearance.

SNOWY TREE CRICKET

Scientific name: *Oecanthus fultoni*
Body length: 1/2 inch
Habitat: Wooded areas, grassland, shrub
Food: Plant matter, insects, aphids
Distribution: Western and northern United States

FAST FACT Crickets are known for their noisy reaction to warm temperatures. On a warm summer night, count a cricket's chirps over a period of 15 seconds, then add 40 to get the temperature in Fahrenheit. Tree crickets are common and often called thermometer crickets.

Jumpers, Hoppers, and Others

Rainforest tree katydid

Katydid

Peacock katydid

Conehead katydid

Mole crickets use their shovel-like forelimbs to burrow underground.

Field cricket

Corn crickets, also known as armored katydids, are covered in sharp spines and can squirt their blood at predators.

Stick insect

Blue-winged grasshoppers are well camouflaged until they take flight.

Leaf insect

Adult horse lubber grasshoppers flash brightly colored wings to threaten predators.

Monkey grasshoppers extend their long legs sideways when at rest.

Differential grasshopper

Bugs freak a lot of people out...a lot! The fear of bugs is called entomophobia. The fear of spiders is called arachnophobia. But most insects aren't harmful to people, and many do a lot of good—from pollinating flowers to keeping the populations of other animals under control. It's helpful to separate the facts from the myths. Some insects, however, can be harmful to crops and dangerous to people.

FACT OR MYTH?

Because people misunderstand some insect behavior, myths have grown over time. Here's the lowdown on which of the best-known fears are true and which are myths.

KILLER BEES ALWAYS ATTACK PEOPLE.

Myth. They typically attack if their nest is disturbed; they don't "hunt" humans. Africanized "killer" honeybees are more dangerous than other bees because nearly all of the colony takes part in the attack and because they are also apt to attack more readily. Only a small percentage of bees from a regular hive would attack in a similar situation.

BUGS CRAWL OR FLY INTO PEOPLE'S EARS.

Fact. Black flies and other gnats commonly fly into people's ears, eyes, and noses, seeking out such places. However, they are not typically doing so to bite people.

EVERY TICK HAS LYME DISEASE.

Myth. Only black-legged ticks carry the disease, according to the Centers for Disease Control and Prevention, and only infected ticks can transmit it. But people should take steps to avoid being bitten when in tick-heavy areas, such as wearing long pants and checking for ticks after being in the woods.

A LADYBUG IS AS OLD AS THE NUMBER OF ITS SPOTS.

Myth. Every species of ladybug has a set number of spots when it is fully mature.

HEAD LICE ARE NOT TRULY DANGEROUS.

Fact. They are annoying and itchy and hard to get rid of, but they don't spread germs that can cause disease.

INSECTS CRAWL OUT OF DRAINS.

Fact. Moth flies can crawl out of drains, and in fact they sometimes breed inside the pipes.

RADIOACTIVITY CAN CREATE GIANT INSECTS.

Myth. Insects will grow only as large as their species type, regardless of exposure to nuclear blasts.

LOCATION, LOCATION

Mosquitoes do pass along infections to millions of people each year, but the majority of these cases are in specific places. Africa is particularly hard-hit by mosquito-carried illnesses such as malaria and yellow fever. One disease that has reached the United States is West Nile virus, with nearly 40,000 cases reported in the U.S. since 1999. State governments are working hard to combat this potentially fatal disease by spraying pesticides and identifying standing water sources where mosquitoes breed.

ON THE FLY

In 2014, a disease resulting from mosquito bites made headlines. More than 800,000 people in the Caribbean developed chikungunya. Spread by mosquitoes, the illness causes fever, cramps, and pain. It is almost never fatal, but it is not fun. Chikungunya is well known in Africa and Asia, so its spread to a new part of the world raised concerns among scientists trying to figure out how it traveled there.

Though insects are an important part of our world, many people are afraid of them. Should they be? There are certainly reasons to be careful around some insects, but they are not always the reasons—or insects—we think.

▶ *Nematodes, as seen through an electron micrograph*

PEST CONTROL

Insects can be a problem when they infest a home or attack crops. When dealing with an infestation of weevils, which can be destructive to plants, gardeners and farmers may release tiny worms called nematodes that are parasitic against the insects. This is called biological control.

Malaria Areas & Risks

| < 0.01 % |
| 0.01–0.1 % |
| 0.1–1 % |
| 1–10 % |
| 10–25% |
| > 25% |

DANGER ZONES

Malaria is widespread in warmer areas, including Sub-Saharan Africa, Asia, and Latin America.

While the vast majority of insects are harmless to humans, some do have the power to hurt or kill people. Most of the deaths come from the disease agents that the insects carry, not from their stings or bites.

TSETSE FLY

The sleeping sickness transmitted by this fly species has killed tens of thousands in recent years, but the annual numbers are coming down, thanks to international efforts to teach people how to control the flies.

JACK JUMPER ANT

These are Australia's most dangerous ants, stinging thousands each year; several people have died from the stings.

MOSQUITO

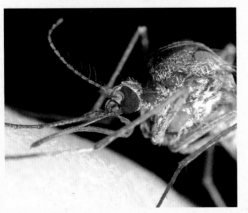

By helping spread malaria and dengue fever, among other diseases, mosquitoes contribute to almost a million deaths each year, making them the deadliest animal on the planet.

SAFARI ANT

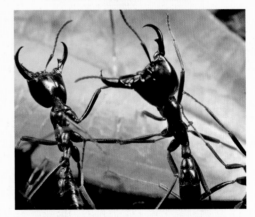

Swarms of 20 million safari ants can inflict great damage to farms, eating crops as they move. Small animals caught in their path don't stand a chance. It's much more rare for them to kill a person, but it's not unheard of.

KISSING BUG

Despite its nice-sounding name, this animal can pack a deadly smack. Kissing bugs, found in Central and South America, can spread a parasite that causes Chagas' disease. More than 100,000 people die annually from Chagas' disease. Kissing bugs are part of a larger family of insects commonly called assassin bugs— this name makes more sense.

FIRE ANT

These fierce social insects sting millions of people each year. The stings cause a painful burning sensation. Death from the stings is rare, but it can happen, especially when the victim has an allergic reaction to insect venom. In 2013, a young football player died after landing on a fire ant nest.

DEADLY TO SOME

While they are not considered among the most deadly insects, bees and wasps cause between 50 and 100 deaths in the United States each year. About 2 million Americans are allergic to the venom in stinging insects. The allergy causes a life-threatening reaction known as anaphylaxis, which affects the whole body and requires immediate medical attention.

Extreme Insects

These stories of record-breaking insects come with a warning: New records are being set all the time, as new discoveries are made. And there are huge numbers of insects that have not been measured yet. But until we know differently, these are the "champs" in a variety of ways.

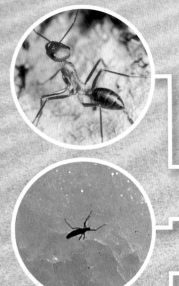

EXTREME SURVIVALISTS

Insects have adapted to just about every environment on Earth. Here are some insects (shown as adults) that can survive extreme conditions.

Saharan desert ants: heat, up to about 120 degrees Fahrenheit

Himalayan midge: cold and dryness, down to about 0 degrees Fahrenheit

Brine fly larvae: saltiness

SMALLEST

Parasitoid wasps are the smallest of the many small insects, at 6/1000 of an inch. It would take two of them to equal a single grain of salt.

MOST MASSIVE

The goliath beetle, at 3.5 ounces (the equivalent of 18 U.S. quarters)

DEADLIEST

Most toxic venom to its prey: the harvester ant, with venom about 20 times as strong as that of a honey bee

Deadliest to humans: the mosquito, which can transmit diseases that kill millions of people each year

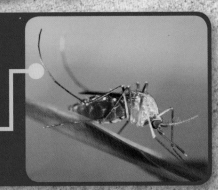

There are millions of types of insects walking, crawling, flying, and squirming around the world. Some of them are bigger, faster, longer, or more amazing than others.

LOUDEST

African cicada, recorded at 106.7 decibels (about as loud as a chain saw or helicopter)

LONGEST LIVED

Most insects live short lives, but a black garden ant queen in captivity lived 28-1/2 years.

FASTEST FLIER

In air: The African desert locust has been clocked flying 21 miles per hour.

GIANT SIZE

The Little Barrier Island giant weta is closely related to crickets. It weighs in at 2.5 ounces.

GIANT WATER BUG

Scientific name: *Lethocerus americanus*
Pronunciation: *leh-THOS-er-us uh-mer-ih-KON-us*
Body length: 2–2-1/2 inches
Food: Insects, small fish, crustaceans, small amphibians and reptiles
Habitat: Pond, marsh, stream
Distribution: Southern Canada to Mexico

FAST FACT The giant water bug uses its long pair of sharp forelegs to capture prey and pull it towards its mouthparts. Watch out for these when walking through shallow streams—they're also called "toe biters."

HEMIPTEROIDS ORDERS

TOTAL SPECIES:
116,775

Psocoptera
(soh-KOP-tuh-ruh)
➡ Book lice
5,574 species

Phthiraptera
(theer-AP-tuh-ruh)
➡ Lice
5,024 species

Thysanoptera
(thye-suh-NOP-tuh-ruh)
➡ Thrips
5,749 species

Hemiptera
(heh-MIP-tuh-ruh)
➡ True bugs
100,428 species

BRENDAN SAYS

Insects are the only animals that have evolved the ability to both live underwater and fly, though most do so at different stages of their lives. Some, like dragonflies and mosquitoes, live underwater as juveniles and take flight as adults. The giant water bug is an example of an insect that can do both as an adult. It can walk on the land, fly, or dive underwater and remain in a pond for weeks. There is hardly anything that stands in its way!

Hemipteroids

AT A GLANCE

It's hard to sum up why the hemipteroids are all in one superorder, since there are more than 100,000 species among them. For starters, let's say that, except for book lice, they are all suckers. That is, they use tubular mouthparts like straws to take in food.

➡ Hemipteroids have been around for about 290 million years.

➡ Hemipteroids are also called Acercaria, which means "without cerci." Cerci are the pair of extra legs, spines, or "fingers" that many other insects have. Hemipteroids don't have these.

➡ They also don't have ocelli (simple eyes) in the nymph stage.

➡ With such a large number of species, hemipteroids live in just about every location and habitat on Earth's surface.

Lice: An Itchy Feeling

The tiny creatures commonly called lice are ectoparasites. That means they live on the outsides of the bodies of other animals. There are more than 5,000 species of lice that live on mammals and birds. They either chew on their hosts or suck their blood. Several kinds of lice live on people. The lice on humans eat by poking their mouths through skin and sucking blood. The places they poke can become very itchy, so if you have lice...you'll usually know it.

BUG BEHAVIOR

Lice are very specialized. Different types of lice live in human head hair and human body hair. Head lice in particular spread easily from head to head, which is why when one person in a class has head lice, other students probably do, too.

NITPICKING

Human head lice lay tiny white eggs called nits on individual strands of hair. They stick to the hair and are hard to wash off. Removing them with a superfine-toothed comb is difficult and time-consuming, but it's the only practical way to get rid of them without shaving the hair off. The term to *nitpick*—meaning to be critical about small things—comes from doing this task.

BRENDAN SAYS

One thing we teach students at ISU is that lice do not live on "fomites," as they're called — the inanimate objects, like clothing, that are on or around people. Bed bugs can and do. But lice, being ectoparasites, require living on the host and are highly adapted for it.

LOUSE GALLERY

No louse (the singular of lice) in this group is bigger than your baby toenail. You might need a magnifying glass to see them in real life.

DID YOU KNOW?

The vast majority of lice are biting lice, not sucking, and they are more annoying than truly harmful. Thankfully, the head lice that can travel from child to child, infesting an entire school classroom, do not serve as a source of infection.

AUSTRALIAN DOG LOUSE

Scientific name: *Heterodoxus spiniger*
Body length: 1/10 inch
Habitat: Dog
Food: Dog flesh and skin
Distribution: Global, except Europe

FAST FACT This insect evolved from one that lives on dingoes in Australia but has since spread to domestic dogs around most of the world.

ELEPHANT LOUSE

Scientific name: *Haematomyzus elephantis*
Body length: 1/9 inch
Habitat: Elephant
Food: Elephant skin
Distribution: Africa, India, Southeast Asia

FAST FACT These tiny insects move from elephant to elephant when the mammals touch skin. Similar lice live only on warthogs.

HOG LOUSE

Scientific name: *Haematopinus suis*
Body length: 1/4 inch
Habitat: Pig
Food: Pig blood
Distribution: Global

FAST FACT Most large mammal groups—horses, rodents, dogs, cows—host their own species of louse. This one lives on pigs.

Not all "bugs" are truly bugs. Only the insects known as true bugs are called bugs by experts. In nearly all cases, if an insect has a name of two or more words, one of which is bug (for example, cabbage plant bug), it is a true bug and a member of this order. When bug is part of a single-word name, though, that species is usually not a true bug. An example is ladybug, which is a beetle.

▶ **LANTERN FLY**
This brightly colored tropical insect is easily recognized by its elongated head.

SUCK IT UP

One thing all true bugs have in common is a mouthpart that sucks up food. Most true bugs eat plant sap or nectar, though others do prey on other insects. But they all have mouths like straws and "eat" only liquid—including the insides of other bugs.

BUG BEHAVIOR

The water scorpion is an aquatic true bug. It has a long tube near its tail that is used as a snorkel. Water scorpions float just below the surface like tiny submarines, waiting for insects or small fish, which they stab with their sharp beaks.

MACRO

Aphids are tiny trouble-makers. They are about one-quarter inch long, and their bright colors provide excellent camouflage around plants and flowers. They tend to feed on plants in large groups, and can do a lot of damage as a result. Their bodies are soft and pear-shaped. Aphids are aggressive— if approached, they will kick their predators. On occasion, they will "stop, drop, and roll" to escape an attacker.

Cicadas live on every continent except Antarctica. They favor warm climates; more than 200 species live in Australia and more than 400 in Africa. And the buzzing of cicadas is the sound of summer in many regions of the United States. The males make loud buzzing sounds as adults, primarily to attract females. Put tens of thousands of these large flying insects together and it's seriously loud!

A cicada can be as much as 2-1/2 inches long when fully grown. As it goes through metamorphosis, it clings to a branch and sheds its exoskeleton. In the photo at right, the adult cicada is emerging from its husk, which remains attached to the tree.

STATS

Cicadas are harmless to people, but the noise some make can damage human ears. At about 100 decibels, the noise of cicadas trying to attract mates can be as loud as a car horn or jackhammer.

SOUND OFF!

Each species of cicada makes its own kind of call, and some species have multiple calls with different meanings. They make the sounds with organs called tymbals, located on their abdomens.

BUG BEHAVIOR

Periodical cicadas make their appearance only every 13 or 17 years. They live underground as nymphs, feeding on sap from tree roots, before emerging. Why do so many emerge from the ground at the same time? Scientists think it helps the species survive to have more individuals than predators can catch at once.

This large group of insects has a wide range of body styles, sizes, and colors.

OLEANDER APHID

Scientific name: *Aphis nerii*
Body length: 1/16–1/8 inch
Habitat: Bush, plant, specifically oleander and milkweed
Food: Plant juices
Distribution: Global, in temperate zones

FAST FACT Aphids' bodies are tiny, but their numbers are not. A female of these fierce garden pests can produce more than a billion eggs in her lifetime.

BEE ASSASSINS

Scientific name: *Apiomerus* (genus)
Body length: 1/2–5/8 inch
Habitat: Garden, field, flowering places
Food: Insects
Distribution: Western North America

FAST FACT Bee assassins get their name for their ability to catch, hold, and stab their favorite prey, bees.

JEWEL BUGS

Scientific name: *Scutelleridae* (family)
Body length: Up to 3/4 inch
Habitat: Plant
Food: Plant juices
Distribution: Global

FAST FACT These insects are from a branch of true bugs known as shield-backed bugs. A covering on the insect's large back closes over the wings when the bug is not in flight. The wide back is also used to shelter eggs.

INSECTS AT WORK

Damselbugs are one of the true bugs that attack other bugs. Their main prey are garden pests such as caterpillars and aphids.

BEDBUG

Scientific name: *Cimex lectularius*
Body length: 1/8 inch
Habitat: Bed, bedding, other indoor places near people
Food: Human blood
Distribution: Global

FAST FACT Bedbugs live close to people—in addition to in beds, they can also be found behind light switch plates and in other small crevices. Their bites leave tiny holes in the skin that become itchy and red.

GREENHOUSE WHITEFLY

Scientific name: *Trialeurodes vaporarium*
Body length: 1/16 inch
Habitat: Garden, greenhouse, field
Food: Plant juices
Distribution: Global

FAST FACT Gardeners hate these insects, which cover many types of home garden plants, chewing into the leaves and stems. They move together from plant to plant, looking like plant dandruff.

FLORIDA LEAF-FOOTED BUG

Scientific name: *Acanthocephala femorata*
Body length: 3/4 inch
Habitat: Wild meadow, grassland
Food: Plant juices
Distribution: Florida

FAST FACT This insect's feet act as camouflage to help it stay hidden from predators. If it does get caught, it can release a really stinky chemical.

Backswimmer

Peanut bug

The greengrocer (a type of cicada) has three simple eyes, called ocelli, between its two large compound eyes.

Buffalo treehopper

Thorn bug

Female cochineal insects gather on cactus plants and feed on the juices, rarely moving unless threatened.

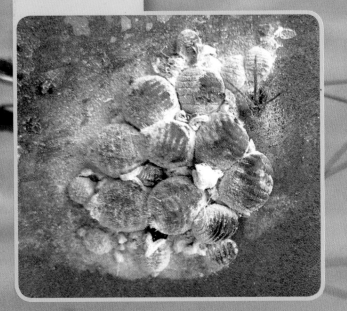

Milkweed bug

Planthopper nymph

Spittlebug nymphs create bubbly white froth to hide from predators while they feed.

Stink bug

Shield-backed bug

Water strider

Ornamental treehopper

This leaf-footed bug has bright colors and slender limbs.

Long-tailed mealybug

Insect vs. Insect

Tens of thousands of insects ride in or on other insect hosts as parasites. Most of those parasites end up causing the deaths of the hosts. Insects that do this are called parasitoids.

NATURE'S MUMMY

Some parasitoid wasps are very particular about where they lay their eggs. The females deposit eggs into tiny stink bug eggs. After an egg hatches, the larva eats the stink bug egg from the inside out. When the larva crawls out to change into an adult, it leaves the empty stink bug egg husk behind—scientists call this husk a mummy.

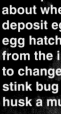

An adult Trissolcus *wasp, after it has emerged from its host.*

A parasite is an organism that lives in or on another organism, which is called the host. The parasite feeds on the host's body, a process that can cause damage to the host. The insect world has many examples of parasites, whether insect on insect or insect on something else.

WORD

A **parasitoid** is a type of parasite that kills its host after living in it or eating it.

This inchworm has parasitoids around its body. While some host insects survive, most are eaten from the inside out by the parasitoid larvae once the eggs hatch.

DINNER TO GO

A type of wasp called jewel cockroach wasp has evolved an interesting way to provide a meal and a home for its young. It lands on the back of a cockroach and injects venom into the cockroach's brain. The wasp can then control the cockroach by moving the cockroach's antennae, like riding a horse using reins, to direct it back to the wasp's home. The wasp then lays an egg on the zonked-out cockroach's abdomen. When the larva emerges, it eats its host.

Insect vs. the World

Insect parasites find more than just other insects to act as hosts. They attach to many different members of the animal kingdom, including humans and other vertebrates. Parasite behavior has evolved as the best way for these organisms to survive—at the expense of others.

EUREKA!

In 2014, scientists at the American Museum of Natural History found a beetle trapped in amber that gave a clue to an amazing discovery. The beetle was a 52-million-year-old ancestor of an ant-loving type of beetle still alive today. No one knew that this beetle-ant relationship was so old! How does the beetle manage its parasitic relationship with the ant colony? It gives off a scent that fools ants into thinking they are safe. The ants then let the beetle into their nest and will even feed the beetle a liquid goo that they make.

PARASITE POWER

Some insect parasites find homes underneath human skin. Sometimes eggs are laid in the skin (bot fly) or larvae burrow into the skin (screwworm) so that the insect lives its entire immature life there, to emerge later as a winged adult. Adults may also invade the skin after living immature life elsewhere (chigoe flea).

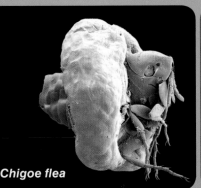

Chigoe flea

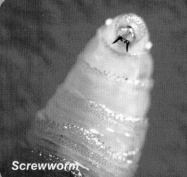

Screwworm

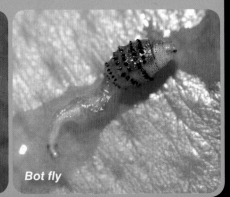

Bot fly

THAT'S DISGUSTING!

Insects are parasites, and they can also become victims of other parasites. One example of this is a Cordyceps fungus that attacks stick insects in Madagascar. The fungus lands on the insect and then attacks by invading the body through the exoskeleton. The bumps shown in the photo are "fruiting," or growing fungus.

THERE'S WORM IN YOUR EYE

One of the really gross parasites that people can acquire is an eye worm called *Loa loa*. If an African deerfly carrying the worms bites a person, the immature worms can hatch inside the human body. The worms live under the person's skin and can even move into the person's eye! *Loa loa* is not an insect, but it could not find a host human without help from one.

Most insects live in habitats filled with plants of one sort or another. They depend on plants as places to hide, find mates, lay eggs, and find food.

TEMPERATE: RAIN FORESTS

Tropical rain forests are home to some of the most amazing and colorful insects in the world. The year-round high temperatures and moist atmosphere are ideal for insects. The thick vegetation of the rain forest creates safe hiding places and a food supply for plant-eating insects, plus it provides hunting grounds for insects seeking other insects.

TEMPERATE: MEADOWS

One estimate of meadowlands in England said that in 1 acre of land, there might be about a ton—2,000 pounds—of insects. Meadow insects live on grasses or in the soil beneath them. They might also find food and shelter in wildflowers. Bees and wasps love such places because they have many flowering plants to feed on. Ants crawl around the stalks of the plants and find lots to eat and share with their colonies.

The place where an animal lives is its habitat. From forests to deserts to meadows and more, insects make their homes in just about every type of habitat on Earth. In fact, insects live everywhere on Earth except in the oceans. Each insect is specialized to live in its particular habitat.

CLIMATE ZONES

- Polar
- Subarctic
- Temperate
- Tropical
- Arid

WORD

Temperate means existing in a middle area between extremes. Much of the United States is in the Northern Hemisphere's Temperate Zone.

TEMPERATE: FORESTS

The huge swaths of trees located in the Pacific Northwest and western Canada are an example of the enormous temperate forests that are home to billions of insects. Other forested areas with moderate temperatures are located in Europe, Russia, and Asia. Every forest has native insects that depend on the trees and the plants in them for food and shelter.

The enormous variety of insects in the world means that they live in a wide variety of habitats. Even in places where conditions are harsh, insects find ways to survive.

ON THE FLY

Insects living high in the Rocky Mountains are causing great damage. A 2014 report by the U.S. Forest Service noted that bark beetles are chewing up trees at a record rate. Holes like those shown here are evidence of bark beetle damage.

THE ARCTIC

The subfreezing world of the northern Arctic region might not seem like a good place for an insect. By some estimates, though, more than 2,000 species of insects and beetles have adapted to the icy terrain above the Arctic Circle. Most find homes in tiny patches of grass or flowers. Amazingly, some of them actually freeze in the soil during winter, emerging in the short summer to eat, mate, and reproduce.

DID YOU KNOW?

Scientists have found only one free-living insect that lives in the Antarctic. The Antarctic midge can survive temperatures down to 5 degrees Fahrenheit.

DESERTS

Hot and dry, deserts present challenges for any animal. But many types of insects thrive in these harsh conditions. Ants build colonies and mounds, crickets and cicadas search for food, and beetles of all sorts dig into the sand to find cooler temperatures and safety.

CROWDED CITIES

Busy urban areas are not good places for wild animals to live, but insects live side by side with people in cities around the world. Cockroaches thrive on human garbage, while flies track down dead animals or rotting food wherever it is left. Silverfish are common sights behind refrigerators or under stoves, and bedbugs simply can't live without humans.

COMMON EASTERN FIREFLY

Scientific name: *Photinus pyralis*
Pronunciation:
  foh-TEE-nuhs pye-RAHL-is
Body length: 1/4–3/4 inch
Habitat: Edge of meadow, field, garden, and yard
Food: Small invertebrates, insect larvae (larval stage only)
Distribution: Eastern United States

FAST FACT A firefly can make a section of its abdomen light up by activating a chemical in its body. The light is used to signal others in its species, usually to attract a mate.

NEUROPTEROIDS ORDERS

TOTAL SPECIES:
366,760

Neuroptera
(nur-OP-tuh-ruh)
➡ Lacewings and relatives
  5,704 species

Coleoptera
(koh-lee-OP-tuh-ruh)
➡ Beetles
  359,891 species

Megaloptera
(meg-uh-LOP-tuh-ruh)
➡ Alderflies, fish flies, and dobsonflies
  337 species

Raphidioptera
(ruh-fid-ee-OP-tuh-ruh)
➡ Snake flies
  225 species

Strepsiptera
(strep-SIPP-tear-uh)
➡ Twisted-wing flies
  603 species

Neuropteroids

AT A GLANCE

If an insect lover studied 10 members of this superorder every day, it would take more than 100 years to study all the species. The beetles alone include more than 350,000 species. Neuropteroids' prehistoric ancestors lived during the Triassic period—more than 200 million years ago— at the same time as the earliest dinosaurs.

➡ In terms of number of species, this is the largest superorder in the insect world.

➡ Nearly all adults in this superorder can fly.

➡ Many species contain the word "fly" in their names but are not actually flies.

➡ Neuropteroids are found on every continent except Antarctica.

BUG BEHAVIOR

Many females in the genus *Photuris*, a different type of firefly than the *Photinus*, pull a nasty trick. They mimic the flashing signals of the *Photinus*. When a male *Photinus* arrives, he finds trouble instead—a hungry predator waiting to eat him. No fair!

These insects sport wings that look like delicate lace. Nearly transparent, the wings have patterns of lines that resemble nets. Gardeners welcome lacewings, as the insects feed on problem insects such as aphids and ants. Some species are so good at destroying pest insects that they are raised by growers and sold to farmers and gardeners to release on their properties. The most recognizable lacewings are greenish in color as adults, but there are others that are brown or have beaded patterns on their bodies.

Green lacewing

SENSITIVE WINGS

Several types of green lacewing have a unique defense against a key predator: the bat. These lacewings can sense the sounds made by bats, which use echolocation to find prey. Lacewings sense these sounds in their wings, helping them avoid the incoming bats.

Bats are a prime lacewing predator.

NO LITTERING!

The lacewing larvae known as aphid lions suck the juices out of tiny aphids, which live on and eat plants. The aphid lions then stack the empty aphid bodies on their backs.

WORD

Making sounds and using their echoes to navigate through air or water is called **echolocation** (*ek-oh-loh-KAY-shuhn*). Dolphins, some whales, and even a few bird species, in addition to bats, use this technique.

BUG BEHAVIOR

When green lacewings lay eggs, they separate each one on its own strand of silk. That's because the larvae will actually eat one another after hatching if they are not kept apart.

Lovely and light, lacewings are the best-known members of Neuroptera, but they also have several interesting-looking cousins. All members of the group have compound eyes, and some of the larvae are fierce and creative predators.

Adult

Larva

ANTLIONS

Scientific name:
Myrmeleontidae (family)
Body size: 1-1/2 inch long;
2–3-inch wingspan
Habitat: Sandy areas, dry soil
Food: Insects
Distribution: Global

FAST FACT Antlion larvae live under soft sand. They create small pits to lure in ants and other insects. When prey falls into the mini-pits, it also falls into the waiting jaws of the antlions.

EASTERN MANTISFLY

Scientific name: *Mantispa sayi*
Body length: 3/4 inch
Habitat: Wooded areas, grassland
Food: Spider eggs (larvae),
insects (adults)
Distribution: Eastern United States

FAST FACT They look like mantises, but they don't act like them. These insects prey on spiders. The larvae can ride a spider's back until the spider makes a nest. Then the larvae moves into the nest, feeding on spider eggs until it is time for metamorphosis.

EASTERN DOBSONFLY

Scientific name: *Corydalus cornutus*
Body length: 2 inches
Habitat: In (larvae)/near (adult) stream
Food: Aquatic creatures (larvae), nothing as adults
Distribution: Eastern North America

FAST FACT With wingspans of as much as 5 inches, dobsonflies are some of the largest insects around. The nasty-looking "horns" of this species are harmless. Their larvae, known as hellgrammites or "go-devils," are popular as models for fishing lures.

OWL FLIES

Scientific name:
   Ascalaphidae (family)
Body length: 1-1/4–1-3/4 inches
Habitat: Field, grassland,
   meadow
Food: Insects
Distribution: Global

FAST FACT These strong fliers are airborne predators similar to dragonflies. Along with their fertilized eggs, female owl flies also lay unfertilized eggs that newly hatched owl fly larvae can eat.

TEXAN SNAKEFLY

Scientific name:
   Agulla adnixa
Body length: 5/8–7/8 inch
Habitat: Forest,
   wooded areas
Food: Aphids, other insects
Distribution: Texas,
   American Southwest

FAST FACT The snakefly gets its name from the long, slender front thorax segment and head, which give it a snakelike appearance.

If the beetles of the world had a family reunion, they'd need an awful lot of space. This is the largest order in the animal kingdom, with more than 350,000 species. With all those species comes enormous variety. However, nearly all beetles have a few things in common. Front wings fold back to create lines that run along the tops of beetle bodies. Beetle mouths are adapted for chewing, not sucking. Beetle antennae come in many lengths and shapes, but each have 11 or fewer segments. Beyond these common traits, the world of beetles is incredibly diverse.

UP FROM GRUBS

Beetles go through complete metamorphosis. That means that the young are very different from adults. The baby beetles all eat a lot; some adult beetles do not eat much, if at all, living mostly to make more beetles. The babies of some beetle species are known as grubs.

TAKING FLIGHT

These photos of a ladybug show how beetles unfold their forewings (1 and 2) to uncover their hind wings. The colorful outer shells are for protection, while the hind wings (3) do the actual flying.

SPOT THE SPOTS

Ladybugs, also known as ladybirds, aren't bugs at all; they're beetles. While they come in different shades and varieties, they are most commonly red, yellow, or orange. Many have spots—as few as two and as many as twenty or more—but some have stripes and others no markings at all. Many ladybug species can, when threatened, bleed from their knee joints. The liquid has a foul smell, so predators might think twice about eating the insects.

Three-banded ladybug

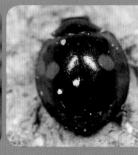
Twice-stabbed ladybug

Fifteen-spotted ladybug

WORD

The insect world is **diverse** because it has a lot of different varieties of insects.

INSECTS AT WORK

Ladybugs are considered good luck in many cultures, and they are the state insect of Delaware, Massachusetts, New York, New Hampshire, North Dakota, Ohio, and Tennessee.

Ladybug on potato leaf

Beetles come in dozens of colors and range in size from nearly microscopic to as big as the palm of your hand. They live in nearly every type of habitat, from sandy to watery, on farmland and in cities. Different species of beetle feed on plants of all kinds, eat other insects, or even dine on dung (animal waste). Some scientists estimate that there might be many, many more undiscovered beetle species "hiding" in the wild.

BRENDAN SAYS

Because of the way their hind wings, which they use to fly, are covered by their hardened forewings, beetles can live in a wide variety of environments. Their wings are protected as they dig in the earth, crawl on the ground, or even swim. Having body armor is a big reason there are so many beetles!

LIFE SIZE

Meet the Hercules beetle, the largest of the rhinoceros beetles at about 6 inches long. Rhinoceros beetles are named for the rhino-like horns protruding from their heads, and the Hercules species is named for its awesome strength.

0   1   2   3   4   5   6   7

LOOK-ALIKES

Many beetles take their common names from other members of the animal kingdom—usually because a body feature or behavior mimics one found in another creature.

Giraffe weevil
→ Long neck like a giraffe
→ Helps it reach plants to eat

Snakefly
→ Named for its elongated appearance
→ Raises its snakelike frontpart to look around

Golden tortoise beetle
→ Wide shell like a tortoise
→ Uses it to shelter babies

Stag beetle
→ Mandibles resemble male deer (stag) antlers
→ Raises them to warn off others

Trilobite beetle
→ Resembles commonly found marine trilobite fossils
→ Lives on land, not water

Rhinoceros beetle
→ Pointed horn resembles that of a rhinoceros
→ Uses it in fighting and digging

There are more than 350,000 species of beetles, with lots of variety among the group. Here are some diverse examples.

GREAT DIVING BEETLE

Scientific name: *Dytiscus marginalis*
Body length: 1 inch
Habitat: Lake, pond, water near ice
Food: Small water creatures, insects
Distribution: Europe, parts of northern Asia

FAST FACT The larvae of these beetles snag prey (a fish, tadpole, or other insect) with sharp jaws, then inject saliva into the animals. The saliva melts the animals' insides, which the larvae then suck out with their strawlike mouths. Bonus cool fact: They can trap air bubbles under their wings to help them stay underwater.

DUNG BEETLE

Scientific name:
  Scarabaeidae (family)
Body length: 1/2–2-1/2 inches
Habitat: Anywhere there is
  animal dung
Food: Dung
Distribution: Global, most
  prominent in Africa

FAST FACT Many dung beetle species lay eggs in dung balls that they roll up. Ancient Egyptians believed dung beetles, also called scarabs, lived among their gods.

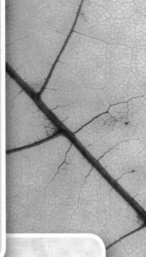

BOLL WEEVIL

Scientific name: *Anthonomus grandis*
Body length: 1/4 inch
Habitat: Wherever cotton is grown
Food: Plants, usually cotton
Distribution: Southern United States,
  northern Mexico

FAST FACT In the early 1900s, boll weevils nearly destroyed America's cotton crop. They ate so much that thousands of farms were shut down. In Georgia alone, in 1914, more than 5 million acres were destroyed.

TEN-LINED JUNE BEETLE

Scientific name: *Polyphylla decemlineata*
Body length: 3/4–1 inch
Habitat: Wood, grassland
Food: Plants
Distribution: Western North America

FAST FACT This is one of many species of insect known as june bugs, though they are actually beetles. The adults are awkward fliers, often crashing into screen doors as they seek light on a summer night. If you see or hear a flying june bug, it's probably a male; females don't usually fly.

WHIRLIGIG BEETLE

Scientific name: *Gyrinidae* (family)
Body length: 1/8–1/4 inch
Habitat: Bodies of freshwater
Food: Insects
Distribution: Global

FAST FACT Clusters of these beetles swim together on the surface of a pond. When disturbed, they spin and move around, sort of like bumper cars, trying to confuse a possible predator.

EYED CLICK BEETLE

Scientific name:
Alaus oculatus
Body length: 1–1-3/4 inches
Habitat: Wooded areas, often around dead trees
Food: Grubs and insects (larvae), nectar (adults)
Distribution: Eastern North America

FAST FACT Using body parts on their undersides, all click beetles can create a clicking sound if threatened. This species also has camouflaging spots on its back that look like eyes.

INSECTS AT WORK

Gardners love ladybugs. Ladybugs can eat hundreds of tiny pest insects, such as aphids, every day.

Golden scarab beetle

Snout beetle

Dogbane leaf beetle

Spotted tortoise beetle

This darkling beetle burrows under the sand of its African habitat to stay cool.

Spotted cucumber beetle

The goliath beetle can grow more than 4 inches long!

Locust borer

Tiger beetle

Japanese beetles feed on the soft parts of leaves, doing harm to plants.

Colorado potato beetle grubs (larvae) can destroy the potato crops they feed on.

Soldier beetle

In fields from medicine to fashion to crime solving, humans have found ways for insects to help out—though it doesn't always turn out well for the insects.

COLOR SOURCE

What do you get when you squish 70,000 cochineal insects? About 1 pound of a bright red dye. It is used in thousands of food products and to color fibers to make clothing.

HEALTHY FLIES... HEALTHY STREAMS

Scientists often look at certain animals as "indicator" species. This means that the presence or absence of the animals indicates whether an environment is healthy or in decline. For example, if a pond or stream has a good variety of species of caddisfly, mayfly, or stonefly, it is probably a good water habitat. But if the insects are absent, that might be a signal that the water is polluted.

Human beings and insects share space in the big, wide world. But insects also have direct roles in people's lives. The study of how humans and insects connect in ways beneficial to humans is called ethnoentomology.

GROSS... BUT HELPFUL

Insect larvae known as maggots eat dead flesh. For centuries, people have used this to help living patients. The maggots of certain insects can be placed onto wounds in the skin. If this is done carefully, under the care of a doctor, the insects eat away the dead flesh around the wound and kill bacteria that can cause infection. This technique is called maggot debridement therapy (debridement means cutting away dead flesh).

Medical maggots are grown in laboratory settings such as this maggot farm.

ON THE FLY

Silkworms have been used for thousands of years to make silk, a highly prized kind of fabric. To get the material used to make silk, people gather silkworm cocoons with the "worms" (they are actually moth pupae, not worms) inside and then boil the cocoons to harvest the silk. The pupae are killed in the process. However, a growing green fashion movement is using "peace silk." Workers harvest the opened cocoons of silkworms only after the moths have completed metamorphosis.

On the Menu

Insects of all sorts play a big part in how human beings eat, whether as a direct food source or as helpers in growing food that is eaten around the world.

POWERFUL POLLINATORS

Bees, butterflies, wasps, and some flies are among the insects that pollinate plants. They carry pollen, needed for plant reproduction, on their legs and bodies as they travel from flower to flower. Insects help more than a third of the world's food crops pollinate, along with nearly every flowering plant.

A GROWING—AND FLYING—INDUSTRY

Farmers in Thailand grew lots of insects in 2014. According to the United Nations, that country has become the world's leader in raising insects for human food. Among the most popular are crickets, grasshoppers, and palm weevils. It could be a sign of the future. To grow a pound of beef, a farmer needs 2,900 gallons of water and 25 pounds of animal feed. To grow a pound of crickets? A gallon of water and just 2 pounds of feed.

PROTEIN POWER

The United Nations put out a report in 2013 that encouraged people to eat insects—a practice known as entomophagy. Insects are less expensive and more readily available than many other food sources, and they are full of protein. There are more than 1,900 species of insects on the menu for people around the world.

PETS LIKE THEM, TOO

Humans are not the only creatures in the average home that might eat insects. Pets such as geckos, frogs, turtles, and even some birds all enjoy a mealworm snack. Mealworms are larvae that become darkling beetles.

Vector Danger!

As insects move from place to place, they can be links between other animals and people. They feed on the blood of animals; the animals they bite sometimes have viruses or other harmful disease-causing agents. The insects become the vectors, or carriers, for viruses, worms, or other microbes. When a disease-carrying insect bites a person, that person might end up catching the disease, too.

NUMBER ONE KILLER

Some types of mosquito carry a tiny protozoan that causes malaria. This tropical disease kills more than 500,000 people a year. Africa is the main location for these deaths, but malaria is found in most tropical areas. There is no cure, although there are some drugs that can ease symptoms. Because it is so widespread, it is a hard disease to fight, but using nets around beds to stop nighttime bites and spraying insecticides can limit the spread of malaria.

A tourist lodge in Madagascar

▶ **A treatment center in Africa**

HITTING HOME

West Nile virus, named for the area in Africa where it was first discovered, is a mosquito-borne illness. Its first appearance in the United States was in New York City in 1999. It can cause fever and rashes and, in severe cases, death. More than 1,700 people in the United States have died from this disease. How is it being fought? Governments use widespread pesticide-spraying programs and work to clean up standing pools of water where the insects breed.

FIGHTING BLINDNESS

Blackflies can infect people with tiny worms that cause a disease called river blindness. Though the disease is present in some South American countries, 99 percent of the cases are in Sub-Saharan Africa. Blackflies breed in streams and rivers, and the worms they pass on do indeed cause blindness in many of the people who are bitten. The Carter Center, an international aid group run by former president Jimmy Carter, is making great strides in fighting river blindness. By distributing medicine and educating people, the Carter Center has cut disease rates. In 2013, Colombia became the first formerly affected country to entirely eliminate river blindness.

Many people around the world are affected by diseases transmitted by insects, and hundreds of thousands of people die from them each year. The fight against these insect-borne illnesses has been going on for a long time.

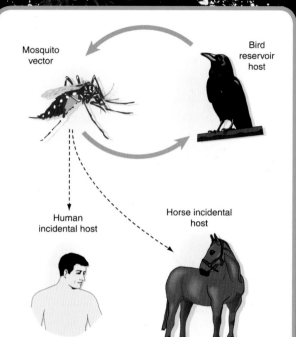

Mosquito vector

Bird reservoir host

Human incidental host

Horse incidental host

WHAT IS AN INSECT VECTOR?

When a mosquito bites a bird that is infected with a virus, as in the case illustrated here, the mosquito can take some of the virus away with it, becoming a vector. Once the insect is a vector, it can transmit the virus to other birds…which can then infect even more mosquitoes. Along the way, the mosquitoes may also transmit the virus to mammals, including humans.

EUREKA!

No one knew what caused malaria until the late 1890s. A British scientist named Ronald Ross discovered the tiny malaria parasite in some mosquitoes and proved that the insects were responsible for passing the parasite to humans. Prevention became easier as a result of this discovery. Ross won the Nobel Prize in Medicine in 1902 for his work on malaria.

LYME, NOT LIME

Bacteria carried by some deer ticks have caused hundreds of thousands of cases of Lyme disease. The illness was named after the town in Connecticut where scientists first identified it in the mid-1970s. Lyme disease affects a person's nervous system; it can also affect blood systems, joints, muscles, and the heart. It is rarely fatal, but it can have a very negative effect on a person's ability to function normally. Experts recommend wearing long pants and sleeves when hiking in the woods, and checking carefully for the presence of ticks after a hike.

MECOPTEROIDS ORDERS

TOTAL SPECIES:
324,634

Mecoptera
(muh-KOP-tuh-ruh)
➡ Scorpionflies
681 species

Siphonaptera
(sye-fuh-NAP-tuh-ruh)
➡ Fleas
2,048 species

Diptera
(DIP-tuh-ruh)
➡ True flies
152,244 species

Trichoptera
(trih-KOP-tuh-ruh)
➡ Caddisflies
12,868 species

Lepidoptera
(leh-puh-DOP-tuh-ruh)
➡ Butterflies and moths
156,793 species

THE INJECTION SECTION

Like many members of this group, a mosquito has a long, thin mouth that it uses like a needle. It stabs this mouthpart, also called a proboscis *(pruh-BAH-suhs)*, into a flower to get nectar or an animal to get blood. Females do the biting, since they must have some blood before their bodies are able to produce eggs.

WORD

Proboscis, used to describe an elongated insect mouthpart, also means nose. An elephant's trunk is a very long proboscis!

Mecopteroids

AFRICAN MALARIA MOSQUITO

Scientific name: *Anopheles gambiae*
Pronunciation: *uh-NOF-uh-leez gam-BYE-ay*
Body length: 1/4 inch
Habitat: Just about anywhere near water
Food: Plant juices (males and females); the blood of animals, including humans (females only)
Distribution: Sub-Saharan Africa

FAST FACT It may be small, but the African malaria mosquito is the most dangerous animal in the world. When it bites a human being, it passes on the germs that cause the disease called malaria. Several hundred million people are infected each year, and more than half a million die from the disease.

AT A GLANCE

Mecopteroids include a wide variety of types of insects, from tiny fleas to massive butterflies and moths. Though they can look very different from one another, mecopteroids share one main thing: similar mouthparts.

➡ All mecopteroids undergo complete metamorphosis.

➡ They have modified mandibles (jaws). Some, including caddisflies and crane flies, don't feed at all. Others use sucking or piercing mouthparts.

➡ Mecopteroids all eat liquid food of one type or another.

➡ Mecopteroids have four to six organs called Malpighian tubules *(mal-PIG-ee-uhn TOO-byools)*. These are the body parts they insects use to let out waste products.

The buzzing of a fly is one of the most common (and annoying) noises heard around the world. Flies are found in every region and every habitat. With more than 150,000 species, they are one of the largest insect orders. Some in this group have sharp, pointed mouthparts that are used to pierce and suck rather than bite. Some flies also use a sponging motion to eat. Flies have large compound eyes that make up most of their heads.

ONE WILL DO

For the most part, insects have two visible sets of wings. On a fly, however, only the front pair is truly formed and visible. The second pair looks more like stubs. These wings vibrate as the animal flies; scientists think this helps keep the insect stable in flight.

BRENDAN SAYS

Flies can be among the most annoying pests to humans, buzzing about and even infecting us with disease agents. But flies are not all bad news. We have learned to use flies to help us in medicine and even in fighting crime. And in the wild, flies reduce waste by eating rotted food.

BUG BEHAVIOR

The larvae of some flies are called maggots. Maggots will eat the dead flesh of other animals. Flies lay their eggs on carcasses so that the larvae that hatch from the eggs will have something to eat.

WORD

The dead body of an animal is a **carcass**.

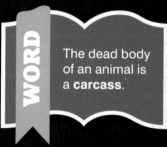

The house fly is the most familiar of the "true flies." But there are other members of this group that don't buzz around as loudly as those particular pests. Crane flies, midges, and gnats each have only two wings, and most have sucking mouthparts, but their overall look is quite different.

COMMON HOUSE FLY

The house fly (*Musca domestica*) is the most common type of fly. It lives for less than a month, and a female can produce close to 1,000 offspring in that short time. The house fly is found all around the world. Some experts estimate that it accounts for 90% or more of all flies found in homes and other human dwellings.

IT'S ALL IN A NAME

Many types of flies eat mainly the blood or juices of a particular kind of animal. Here are some named for what they eat.

BEE FLIES

Not only do they look like bees, their maggots live and feed in bees' nests.

HORSE FLIES

When a horse shakes its mane or swishes its tail, it may be shooing off these flies.

THE MIGHTY MIDGE

Midges are often felt before they are seen. Like mosquitoes, many types of midges feed on human or animal blood. Midges are smaller and quieter than mosquitoes. Their tiny size (shown in close-up here) and stealthy attack have earned them the nickname "no-see-ums."

Crane flies look like oversized mosquitoes. They have very long legs, but are not good fliers.

DEER FLIES

Only the females bite and suck blood; they also feed on rabbits and rodents in addition to deer.

APHID FLIES

Good for gardens, these flies' larvae eat aphids, the tiny insects that destroy plants.

MYDAS FLIES

Larvae eat a variety of insects underground or on/in the soil, and the females may lay eggs in ant nests so that their larvae have a ready food supply.

What's all the buzz about? It's about this group that includes some noisy insects that are well-known to many people, and also shows off some amazing examples of insect evolution.

NEW ZEALAND GLOWWORM

Scientific name:
  Arachnocampa luminosa
Body length: 1/2 inch
Habitat: Waitomo Caves and others, New Zealand
Food: Flying insects (larvae only)
Distribution: New Zealand

FAST FACT The larvae of this glowworm are bioluminescent, meaning that they glow. They cling to the cave ceilings and dangle sticky strands of silk to capture insects to eat. This eerie display has made the caves where they live a popular tourist destination.

NORTHERN CADDISFLY

Scientific name: *Hydatophylax argus*
Body length: 3/4 inch
Habitat: Small bodies of water
Food: Plants, organic matter (larvae); plant sap or nectar, if anything (adults)
Distribution: Northeastern United States

FAST FACT Caddisfly larvae are key food sources for fish, and many fishing lures are made to imitate their movement. Caddisfly lures are often used when fishing for trout.

STALK-EYED FLY

Scientific name:
  Diopsidae (family)
Body length: 1/2 inch
Habitat: Rain forest
Food: Unknown
Distribution: Papua New Guinea

FAST FACT The eyes are at the tips of the eyestalks of these flies, and they are as much as 2 inches apart, giving stalk-eyed flies the largest head among flies. The stalks are used in battles for mates.

ROBBER FLY

Scientific name:
Asilidae (family)
Body length: 3 inches
Habitat: Rain forest
Food: Insects
Distribution: Global

FAST FACT Robber flies land on the backs of other species and suck out their insides. They can even do this in midflight!

INSECTS AT WORK

Crime scene experts called forensic entomologists study the eggs and maggots of blow flies. Blow flies smell dead bodies and quickly land to lay their eggs. The number, location, age, and size of the maggots on a body can help the experts determine the time of death.

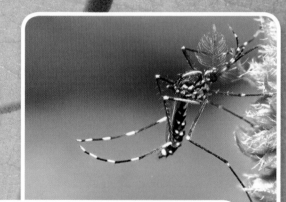

TACHINID FLIES

Scientific name: *Tachinidae* (family)
Body length: 1/8–1/2 inch
Habitat: Meadow, flower field
Food: Nectar (adults)
Distribution: Global

FAST FACT A tachinid fly lays eggs in, on, or near caterpillars and other bugs. When the larvae hatch, they eat the caterpillar, feeding until fully grown.

ASIAN TIGER MOSQUITO

Scientific name: *Aedes albopictus*
Body length: 1/4 inch
Habitat: Areas near freshwater
Food: Nectar (adult males), nectar and animal blood (adult females)
Distribution: Asia; southern United States as an invasive species

FAST FACT The Asian tiger mosquito has a long, thin mouth that it uses like a needle. It stabs its proboscis" into a flower to get nectar or into an animal to get blood.

A dog may be a person's best friend, but a flea is definitely not a dog's (or a cat's) best friend. The cat flea (*Ctenocephalides felis*) lives on the skin and amid the hair of dogs and cats, as well as other mammals. There is also a dog flea, which is much less common in the United States. Other types of fleas live on birds and rodents. A flea's body is almost flat vertically—that is, it's flat from side to side instead of flat like a pancake. This helps it slip between strands of an animal's thick hair or feathers. Fleas' legs have hooks and barbs that make them hard to scrape or brush off.

BRENDAN SAYS

Fleas like dogs and other vertebrates (including humans) because they are warm and provide food and shelter at the same time.

BUG BEHAVIOR

Most flea species will aim for a particular type of animal. The insects have claws that help them grip the animal's skin or hair. Bristly hairs and spines help them stay on an animal even when it's moving.

Dog flea in fur

FLEA GALLERY

It's a good thing that these photos of fleas are much bigger than life size. Fleas are so tiny that you need big pictures to see all the details. But imagine if fleas were really this big—dogs and cats (and other animals they infest) would be really, really uncomfortable.

ORIENTAL RAT FLEA

Scientific name: *Xenopsylla cheopis*
Body length: 1/10 inch
Habitat: Rodents, people, rodent nests, human dwellings
Food: Blood (adults), organic matter (larvae)
Distribution: Global

FAST FACT This flea has been traced to the spread of diseases in humans, including the plague.

STICKTIGHT FLEA

Scientific name:
Echidnophaga gallinacea
Body length: 1/10 inch
Habitat: Poultry farm
Food: Organic matter (larvae)
Distribution: Global

FAST FACT These fleas are major pests for chickens and other poultry.

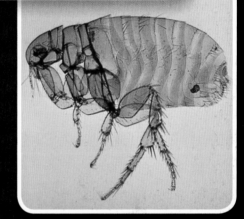

FLEA-BITTEN

How can you tell if a dog has fleas? Frequent scratching, licking, and biting its ears or other areas of its body may indicate that Fido is infested. The best way to check is to part the fur and look for little black specks. These are bits of flea excrement known as "flea dirt." Flea combs, with teeth close together, can remove the specks and live fleas. But that's just the first step in ridding your dog, and home, of these irritating pests, and you may need to call in a vet or other expert for help.

Butterfly Bonanza

Butterflies are found in habitats around the world, and they are among the most familiar insects. The majority of butterflies have long and slender bodies, with straight antennae that end in small bulbs called clubs. But they are perhaps best known for their dazzling array of colors, patterns, and shapes.

Buckeye butterfly

Southern comma butterfly

Red admiral butterfly

Swallowtail butterfly

Birdwing butterfly

Helena morpho butterfly

Large copper butterfly

Lemon emigrant butterfly

MACRO

From a distance, a butterfly's wings show patterns of colors. The patterns help members of each species recognize one another. A close-up look at a monarch butterfly wing (shown below) shows that these patterns are made up of overlapping scales.

FAMOUS BABIES

Caterpillars are colorful and diverse, too, with a variety of patterns, spines, spikes, and fuzz.

Swallowtail caterpillar

Postman caterpillar

Wooly bear caterpillar

Golden birdwing caterpillar

0   1

LIFE SIZE

The Queen Alexandra's birdwing is the largest butterfly in the world. Its body is 3 inches long, and it has a 10-inch wingspan. This butterfly is an endangered species, with a shrinking population due to habitat destruction in its native Papua New Guinea.

3   4   5   6   7   8   9   10

Monarchs: Winged Beauties

One of the most familiar butterflies in North America is the orange-and-black monarch. The caterpillars of this type of butterfly eat only milkweed plants. Over time, toxins from that plant build up inside the caterpillar, becoming part of the butterfly after metamorphosis. This makes the monarch poisonous to nearly all predators. Over millions of years, several species have evolved to mimic, or copy, the monarch's coloring. In this way, other orange-and-black butterflies avoid danger even though they are not poisonous themselves.

PACK OF 'FLIES

Monarchs migrate great distances from Canada to Mexico. At each end of the journey, and at points in between, they gather in very large numbers in very small areas. Tens of thousands might pack onto a single tree branch. They are so numerous that nearby listeners can hear the collective flapping of wings.

IN DISGUISE

As either caterpillars or adults (or both), some butterflies and moths have evolved with colors, patterns, or shapes that help them evade predators.

Common brimstone butterfly
This butterfly looks like a leaf, but it isn't.

Angle shades moth
Tree bark makes a great place to hide in plain sight for this moth.

> Monarch butterflies and milkweed need one another for survival. When a butterfly lands on a milkweed plant, it collects pollen on its legs while it eats. The pollen is then deposited on the next plant visited. This process pollinates plants so they can reproduce. This type of relationship between two different species is called mutualism.

Viceroy butterfly
Colors and pattern mimic the monarch, making it look poisonous to predators.

Cloudless sulphur butterfly
This butterfly's light-colored wings make it hard to spot on sun-dappled flowers or plants.

Hawk moth caterpillar
This caterpillar warns off predators with its snakelike look.

Though often confused with butterflies, moths are different animals. Some moth antennae are bushy or look like small fans. Their bodies are usually plump and fuzzy. They have two pairs of wings, but in most cases they are not as colorful as butterflies. At rest, they often spread their wings out, whereas butterflies often hold their wings above their backs. Moths are nearly all nocturnal animals, whereas butterflies are active during the day. Often thought of as pests, fabric-eating moths can destroy sweaters and linens, and an infestation of gypsy moths can devour the foliage of trees and shrubs.

Moth with fanned, bushy antennae

LIFE SIZE

Atlas moth cocoons reach an average size of 4-1/2 inches.

One of the insect world's biggest wingspans belongs to a moth. The Atlas moth, which lives for only a few days after emerging from its cocoon, can have a wingspan that is a foot across.

LIGHT SEEKERS

Have you ever tried to dodge a bunch of moths hovering by the entrance light when you go into a building at night? Scientists aren't sure why moths are drawn to lights. Some think that it is because moths use celestial navigation, relying on the moon and stars. Others think they are searching for the morning light, which lets these nighttime fliers know it is time to sleep.

TENT CATERPILLARS

Named for the tent-like nests they build in their larval stage, several species have one thing in common: a voracious appetite that can strip the leaves off trees, causing permanent damage.

▶ **INCH BY INCH** In one moth family, each juvenile starts out as a well-known caterpillar: the inchworm. An inchworm moves by walking its back end toward its front, then walking its front end away from its back, seeming to measure the earth in inches. Its family name is Geometridae, from the Latin *geometer* (*geo* means earth and *meter* means measure.)

For variety of color and pattern, no insect group can beat the butterflies. And though moths aren't as colorful, they do have a wide variety of interesting scale patterns.

GLASS WING

Scientific name: *Greta oto*
Body length: 3/4 inch
Habitat: Forest, garden, meadow
Food: Plant nectar
Distribution: Mexico, Central America

FAST FACT Without colored scales, the wings are almost completely transparent. Predators can barely spot this see-through insect.

INDONESIAN OWL MOTH

Scientific name:
Brahmaea hearseyi
Body length: 2 inches
Habitat: Forest
Food: Leaves, plants (caterpillars); nectar (adults)
Distribution: Southeast Asia

FAST FACT The coloring on the upper side of this butterfly's wings mimics the look of an owl's feathers. The caterpillar boasts a fierce-looking set of curving horns.

COTTONWOOD CROWN BORER MOTH

Scientific name: *Sesia tibialis*
Body length: 1-1/2 inches
Habitat: Forest
Food: Woody plants (caterpillars), plant nectar (adults)
Distribution: Western North America

FAST FACT This moth looks very much like a hornet and is sometimes referred to as the American hornet moth. It can be destructive to young willow and poplar trees.

INSECTS AT WORK

Monarch butterflies are ambassadors of the insect world. Because of their wide range and familiar colors, as well as shrinking population, monarchs are used as a flagship species in conservation efforts. The story of monarchs' long migration and their importance as plant pollinators helps raise awareness of other animals and plants that need help.

BLUE MORPHO

Scientific name: *Morpho peleides*
Body length: 1-1/2 inches
Habitat: Tropical forest
Food: Leaves, plants (caterpillars); plant sap, rotting vegetation (adults)
Distribution: Central America, Mexico

FAST FACT The top of this butterfly is bright blue, while the underside is brown with spots. When it flutters, the flashing difference between the blue and brown confuses predators. Blue morphos can have wingspans wider than 5 inches.

DINGY SKIPPER

Scientific name: *Erynnis tages*
Body length: 1/2 inch
Habitat: Grassy areas, often in sunlight
Food: Plant nectar
Distribution: Global, in temperate zone

FAST FACT Skippers are a type of butterfly named for their flitting, bouncing flight style. Their muted colors help them camouflage on the ground, where they bask in the sun.

NEGLECTED EIGHTY-EIGHT

Scientific name: *Diaethria neglecta*
Body length: 1-1/2 inches
Habitat: Rain forest
Food: Rotting fruit, nectar
Distribution: Central and South America

FAST FACT Named for the pattern on their wings, which resembles the number "88" (and sometimes an "89"), this diurnal butterfly likes to bask in the late afternoon sun before settling in to sleep.

When Cairns birdwings fold their wings, they show different colors and patterns.

Flower fly

Rosy maple moth

Madagascan sunset moth

Silkworms and moths are commonly bred for their silk by people worldwide.

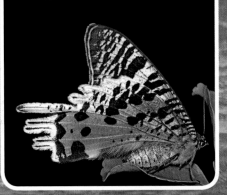

Zebra longwing butterflies use their proboscis to collect pollen from flowers.

Long-legged fly

Lobster moth

The Morgan's sphinx moth has the longest proboscis, at up to 14 inches long.

Cecropia caterpillars are big—up to 5 inches long!

Yellow fly

Luna moth

Scorpionfly

The gypsy caterpillar and moth are among the biggest pests in the eastern United States.

Insects that are predators must capture prey to survive. Insects that rely on animals as a food source may sneak up on prey, lie in wait for passing targets, or rampage over the landscape. Some insects are scavengers, and eat the dead remains of other animals.

SMALL BUT FIERCE

In 2011, two scientists in Israel discovered some bad news for frogs. Amphibians like to eat the larvae of beetles from the genus *Epomis*. The problem is, the larvae also like to eat the frogs. The researchers watched as larvae wiggled their antennae to attract frogs. When frogs tried to eat them, larvae grabbed on and start eating, as shown here.

A TRAP IN THE SAND

Antlion larvae create tiny but deadly pits in sand. They burrow into the soft ground, leaving small openings above them. When an ant wanders into the hole, the antlion waiting below snags it and devours it.

Insects that eat other insects use a wide variety of tactics to attack and capture prey. Meanwhile, prey insects rely on a host of defensive moves, against both fellow insects and other predators.

DISGUISE AND ATTACK

Ambush predators often attack prey while camouflaged. Several types of insect hunt this way. Camouflage protects the insects from predators as well. Some assassin bugs are masters of disguise—they carry ant carcasses on their back to confuse prey and predators, who end up with a mouth full of dead ants while the assassin bug escapes.

FIGHTING FOR A MATE

Some beetles battle not for food but for territory or a mate. A rhinoceros beetle uses its large horn to flip rivals. Male stag beetles also use their mandibles like giant pincers rather than like flippers. And male stalk-eyed flies use their eyestalks to wrestle with one another.

Rhinoceros beetles

Stag beetles

Stalk-eyed flies

Insects are prey for animals of all sorts, including other insects. They have evolved strategies to avoid being eaten. Flying away is the first move for most adult insects. Or they run, if they are fast enough to escape that way. But some insects can't move quickly enough to elude predators (or they don't need to), so they have other defensive tactics.

SPEW? EW!

Bombardier beetles are well known for spraying stinky goo when people pick them up. They're not the only insects that use liquid as a chemical defense. Ladybugs ooze blood from their knees; some termite soldiers send out a sticky goo that can freeze a predator in its tracks; and some cockroaches put out gluelike stuff that stops ants that are attacking them.

Bombardier beetle

A HONEYBEE HEAT BALL

Bees are known for stinging in defense. Some honeybees in Japan use another form of defense when a hornet attacks their colony. Instead of stinging, the bees turn up the heat. The tiny bees swarm around the hornet in a tight ball. The tightly packed bees vibrate. This raises the hornet's body temperature by several degrees and it overheats and dies. The photo at right shows what experts call a hot defensive bee ball—the yellow is the hornet—and the thermograph, which measures heat, shows the elevated temperature.

HIDING IN PLAIN SIGHT AND STANDING OUT TO SURVIIVE

When they can, insects will evade their predators using camouflage, hiding among natural elements such as sticks, leaves, bark, or flowers.

Other insects use mimicry as a defense. This clearwing moth looks like a more dangerous wasp, which helps keep predators away.

Leaf butterfly looks like…a

AMERICAN PELECINID WASP

Scientific name: *Pelecinus polyturator*
Pronunciation: *pel-uh-SEE-nuhs pah-lee-TOOR-uh-tor*
Wingspan: 2-1/2 inches
Food: Beetle grubs (larvae), plant nectar (adults)
Habitat: Areas of soft soil
Distribution: Eastern United States

FAST FACT The female of the species uses its long, thin abdomen to locate beetle grubs and deposit its eggs. This doesn't work out well for the grubs, which are eaten by the wasp larvae when they hatch.

BUG BEHAVIOR

The tarantula hawk is an example of a spider wasp. It gets its name from its favorite prey—tarantulas. Though smaller than most tarantulas, the female has a long stinger and can overcome a spider. The wasp then leaves the spider for its young to eat.

HYMENOPTEROIDS ORDERS

TOTAL SPECIES:
144,695

Hymenoptera
(hye-muh-NOP-tuh-ruh)
➡ Ants, bees, wasps, and sawflies
144,695 species

AT A GLANCE

The large order called Hymenoptera covers a lot of ground in the insect world and includes some of the insects that people find most familiar. In fact, this order is associated with a lot of *mosts*: It includes some of the most numerous insects in the world, and some of the most scary, too. Some estimates say that 10 percent of all the animals in the world are part of Hymenoptera.

➡ They are often social insects, usually living together in large colonies or nests.

➡ The life of the nest centers around a queen.

➡ Some species—especially wasps, bees, and hornets—are known for their stings, which can be quite painful to humans.

➡ Insects in this order have two pairs of wings, with the rear set usually smaller.

➡ In bees, ants, and wasps, the bodies narrow sharply between thorax and abdomen—a form called a pedicel.

➡ Insects in Hymenoptera have four stages in their lives—egg, larva, pupa, and adult—and undergo complete metamorphosis.

Ants are among the most recognizable types of insect. In nearly all ant species, their three body parts are easily identified. Most have long legs, and their antennae have "elbows," or bends, in them. Within a species, the ants that can mate are able to fly, while others cannot. Ants are also some of the most widely distributed animals on Earth. They live on every continent except Antarctica and thrive in nearly every type of climate and terrestrial habitat.

CLOSE QUARTERS

Ants are social creatures that live together in large colonies. Different types of ants build various kinds of homes. Some live underground, some build nests just above the ground, some construct large anthills, some make homes high up in trees, and some nest in wood, including tree stumps and buildings.

Above the ground

Underground

Tree stump

In a tree

In a mound

SPEED RECORD

Trap-jaw ants have the fastest mouths in the insect world, and the fastest strike in the animal kingdom. Using a kind of latch system to hold their mouths open and then release them at a high speed and rapid acceleration, they can snap their jaws together at up to 145 miles per hour. Trap-jaw ants can also use that snapping power to propel themselves into the air to escape a predator.

ON THE FLY

A study published in 2014 showed that ants can be very helpful in cleaning up litter. Conducted in New York City, the study looked at which ants would eat the most: ants in a park setting, or ants on a city street. The street ants ate more than twice as much as those in the park.

SMALL BUT MIGHTY

Ants are tiny, but they are enormously strong. A typical leaf-cutter ant, for example, can lift a piece of plant matter 50 times its own body weight. An equivalently strong human would be able to lift a pickup truck over his or her head.

If you see one ant, you will probably see a lot more. Like many of the insects in this group, ants are social animals. They live their whole lives together in groups called colonies, usually in underground nests that are home to millions of other ants. In an ant nest, individual ants have different jobs. There is one queen ant, whose job is to produce offspring. There are worker ants that build the nest and gather food. There are soldier ants that protect the nest; they are often larger in size. All these different ants, with different jobs, work together to help the entire colony survive and thrive.

▶ *Queen ant*

TEAMWORK

Ants around the world are known for being hard workers and good teammates. They work together to accomplish tasks too difficult for a single ant.

Leaf-cutter ants
Together, they cut out small pieces of leaves and carry them back to the colony. A fungus on the leaves feeds the colony.

Weaver ants
They work together to make silk nests to protect their queen and her eggs.

BUG BEHAVIOR

Some ant species have a type of worker called a super major. These individuals have heads much larger than the other ants in the nest do. They are used as soldiers to repel attacks. Their heads can even block the entrance to the nest, preventing enemies from entering.

Super major compared to minor ant

CHEMICAL COMMUNICATION

How do ants in a colony communicate with one another? Through chemical compounds known as pheromones. Each pheromone has the same meaning to all members of a species. So ants can sense or smell pheromones in the air that tell them where to find food, whether an enemy is coming, or if it's time to move the colony.

Army ants
Named for their mass movements across a landscape, they eat whatever gets in their way.

Aphid-herding ants
Some ants tend "flocks" of aphids. In return for food, the ants help keep the aphids safe.

Fire ants
Many ants link their bodies together, forming small bridges or rafts to keep safe when it floods.

Bees have an enormous impact on the world's ecosystem. Along with providing honey and beeswax, they are responsible for the pollination of many types of plants. For plants to reproduce, they need pollen. Bees spread that pollen from flower to flower as they buzz around feeding. (It sticks to their bodies.) This helps plant species—including trees, crops, fruit, and flowers—thrive. Most bees take the plant pollen and nectar they feed on back to their hives to share with their colonies. Most people are familiar with the honeybee and the bumblebee; there are also more than 25,000 other species of bee.

COLONIAL COLONY

English settlers who founded the Jamestown colony brought honeybees to North America. The settlers wanted the bee colonies to help them carry on their farming in the New World.

BUG BEHAVIOR

Bees generally do not sting unless they are attacked or bothered. But an aggressive breed of bee known as the killer bee was created when Brazilian farmers, hoping to increase their honey crops, bred African bees with local bees. The farmers did not get the tame result they expected. The new killer bees attacked in large groups when bothered, instead of in small groups like other honeybees do. In such large swarms, these bees can kill animals or people.

WORD

Pollination means giving a plant the pollen it needs in order to reproduce. In the wild, this is often done by bees and insects.

BRENDAN SAYS

Bees don't seek out people. We just happen to be in their flight paths or around the flowers or drinks that they seek for food. But a person will often become scared and start swatting at a bee that gets close. Most of the time, the bee will leave, but there is a possibility it will sting. The lesson: Don't provoke bees if you can help it!

A HAPPY DANCE

After a honeybee scout finds a good source of pollen, it returns to the hive to spread the word. Scientists have discovered that the movement patterns of these returning bees form a "dance" as they walk and vibrate in the hive. The movements show the other bees the direction and distance of the new pollen source.

Wasps: A Nesting Instinct

Like ants and bees, many types of wasps are social animals. The shapes and styles of the nests that they build, however, are much more diverse than those of ants or bees. Wasps are builders, and they use plant fibers and juices their bodies produce to make a kind of paste to hold their structures together. Working first as individuals and later as a group, they build a wide array of nest shapes and forms to live in. Some wasps pack food—such as paralyzed caterpillars or other insects—into their nests for emerging larvae to feed on.

CONSTRUCTION SITES

Wasps are industrious builders, and different species build different kinds of nests from a variety of substances.

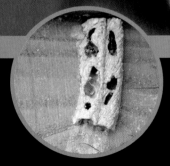

Potter wasp
Uses balls of mud to build small nests that look like vases with narrow necks.

Organ pipe mud dauber
Creates muddy half tubes on the surfaces of trees, wood fences, or buildings.

DINNER FOR ONE

Many wasps live the early part of their lives as parasites on other animals, usually other insects. The female wasp has an ovipositor—a kind of egg injector—that she uses like a stinger to lay an egg or eggs inside the host. When the larvae emerge from the eggs, they eat the host insect from the inside out. A caterpillar is a common host for wasp eggs.

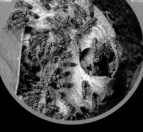

South American polybia wasp
Builds ball-like nests.

Paper wasp
Constructs nests with hexagon-shaped chambers inside for laying eggs.

Yellowjacket
Some yellowjacket species build nests underground.

Ants, bees, and wasps are the only insects armed with stingers. But within that group, there's a great variety of body styles and colors.

GIANT ICHNEUMONS

Scientific name: *Megarhyssa* (genus)
Body length: 1–1-1/2 inches
Habitat: Dead tree
Food: Grubs or larvae of other insects (larvae only)
Distribution: North America

FAST FACT These wasps use their long tails to drill holes into trees, then lay their eggs on spiders or other insects inside. The larvae eat the other insects after emerging from their eggs.

RED FIRE ANT

Scientific name:
Solenopsis invicta
Body length: 1/4 inch
Habitat: Soil, sandy areas
Food: Plant and animal matter
Distribution: South America, southern and western United States

FAST FACT
Fire ants have painful stings and can cause deadly allergic reactions in some people. This is an invasive species that is spreading rapidly.

WESTERN YELLOWJACKET

Scientific name:
Vespula pensylvanica
Body length: 1/2 inch
Habitat: Underground, under buildings
Food: Insects, flesh of dead animals, nectar
Distribution: Western North America

FAST FACT Yellowjackets don't like cold weather. Except for egg-laying females, all yellowjackets die out each winter.

VELVET ANTS

Scientific name:
Mutillidae (family)
Body length: 1/2–1 inch
Habitat: Desert, dry ground
Food: Host insects (larvae), plant nectar (adults)
Distribution: Global

FAST FACT Not actually ants, these are wasps that lay their eggs in nests. One species is commonly called the cow killer, but though its sting is painful, it can't actually kill such a large animal.

HONEYPOT ANT

Scientific name: *Myrmecocystus mimicus*
Body length: 1/3 inch
Habitat: Underground desert areas
Food: Other insects, dead insects, nectar
Distribution: Southwestern United States

FAST FACT Some honeypot ants hang from the top of the nest and fill up with honeydew (a syrupy substance produced by aphids). Their abdomens balloon to many times their original size to store the nectar, which then provides food for others in the nest.

LONG-HORNED BEES

Scientific name:
  Eucerini (tribe in the family Apidae)
Body length: Varies by species; most less than 1/2 inch
Habitat: Farm, field
Food: Flower nectar
Distribution: North and South America

FAST FACT They don't have horns, but these bees do have very long antennae which help them seek out a wide variety of plants that they pollinate, including squashes and sunflowers.

BLACK-HEADED ASH SAWFLY

Scientific name: *Tethida barda*
Body length: 1/2 inch
Habitat: Forest, ash tree
Food: Ash tree leaves (larvae), tree sap (adults)
Distribution: Eastern United States

FAST FACT Sawflies eat the leaves of the ash trees for which they're named. They're very small, and when threatened by a predator, they pretend to be dead.

Queen
weaver ant

Emerald cockroach wasp

Weaver ants, known for their teamwork, build nests by pulling leaves together.

Some bees create tunnel-like nests underground in sandy soil.

Golden carpenter ant

Red and black mason wasp

A bite from a bulldog ant, found in Australia, is said to be one of the most painful, and can be deadly.

Paper wasp

Leafcutter bee

A German yellowjacket is easily identified by the three tiny black dots on its face.

Mud dauber wasp

Cuckoo wasp

Wood ant

Army ant

Potter wasps eat caterpillars and help keep their population in check.

Insects Are My Business

From the lab to the field, here are some of the most popular jobs working with insects.

Scientists who study bugs are **entomologists**. They have college degrees, usually in biology or entomology. Most also go to graduate school to learn more about insects and earn advanced degrees. Entomologists may work in labs, at companies that use insects, or at universities or museums doing research on insect topics.

Forensic entomologists are experts who study how insects live on and around dead bodies. They also look at other insect evidence that can point investigators to solutions. These scientists have become an important part of law enforcement. It's not pretty work, but it can help catch criminals.

The fruit fly is a main lab partner for **genetic researchers.** Because of the fly's short life, it is a great study aid when scientists investigate genetics— the science of how traits are passed down to offspring and change. Researchers use many generations of fruit flies to experiment with heredity, DNA, and other genetics topics.

BRENDAN SAYS

There is always something new to discover about insects! I remind myself of this every day at work. It lets me know that I'm working toward something that is important and worth investigating for the rest of my life.

A special kind of pest control is called **vector management.** A vector is an organism that transmits disease. In the insect world, that is often a mosquito. Most county and state governments have departments that specialize in vector management. The workers in those departments try to protect people from mosquitoes and other insects that carry disease. They try to eliminate mosquito breeding grounds, and they spray chemicals that chase the insects away.

Knowing how to get rid of bugs can lead to a steady career in **pest control**. Experts in pest control, also known as exterminators, kill bugs that are bothering or endangering humans. Pest control workers have to know a lot about insects, including what they eat and where they live as well as how they behave. Insects such as cockroaches, termites, ants, and bedbugs—which have infested many cities in recent years—can be targets of pest control, as can spiders.

If you love bugs, you can make them part of your working life in many ways. For some careers, you will need to attend many years of school. But other jobs take only some initial training, and then you can learn as you work.

THE ACTING BUG

When a movie or TV script calls for a cockroach invasion or locusts to land on cue, the producers call for an **insect wrangler.** Insect wranglers collect insects and bring them to set. Insects can't be trained like other animal actors, but these experts can coax roaches and other insects to do a few simple things. A wrangler also makes sure the cast and crew don't bother the insects…and vice versa! When the shoot is over, the wrangler collects all the insects and takes them away.

Steve Kutcher, shown at left and above, is an entomology consultant for the entertainment industry. He has developed techniques to make various bugs act on cue, and once made a live wasp fly into an actor's mouth. Films he worked on include *Arachnophobia*, *Jurassic Park*, and *We Bought a Zoo*.

This millipede is ready for its close-up!

Tracking Mosquitoes

Brendan's lab is located at Iowa State University in Ames, Iowa. The goals of his Iowa Mosquito Surveillance Lab are to track mosquitoes and to find out which ones are spreading disease. The first step—catching mosquitoes!

1 COLLECTION

Brendan and his team visit local places known to be mosquito breeding grounds. They look for standing water, where they find immature, aquatic forms of the insects. To collect adult insects, they choose traps based on whether the insects are looking for blood before laying eggs or are already in the egg-laying stage. Lights help attract the bugs at night, too.

2 TRANSPORT

Once the bugs are caught, they make the ride to the lab. The team transports them in special cases that prevent escape while still keeping the insects alive.

3 EXAMINATION

Special instruments called forceps (*FOR-seps*) are used to hold tiny insects, so they can be examined closely.

BRENDAN SAYS

By tracking mosquitoes every day, we are able to keep our fingers on the pulse of that insect population. Our research can help direct efforts to limit the spread of disease, so that makes the hours spent tramping in the woods and peering into microscopes all worth it.

Brendan Dunphy, the *Bugopedia* insect expert, is hands-on with insects year-round. Certain times of the year are devoted to an important research project. It's called insect surveillance, and its aim is to track mosquitoes in his area.

4

IDENTIFICATION

Brendan can tell which species a mosquito is just by looking at it. His team almost always needs a microscope for a closer look.

5

FREEZING

To preserve the insects for testing, Brendan puts them in the freezer. This keeps the insects' bodies and any viruses they are carrying from decomposing.

6

TESTING

Brendan and his team want to know if these mosquitoes are infected with anything that can cause disease in people, such as West Nile virus. To find out, they send out frozen specimens for molecular testing.

7

DATA ENTRY AND GRAPHING

All the information the team gathers goes into a huge database. The information is turned into handy graphs and charts. This is important for figuring out what the data means. Some of the charts show how many mosquitoes are in the area. Others track the spread of disease. Officials throughout Iowa use this information to help keep people and animals healthy.

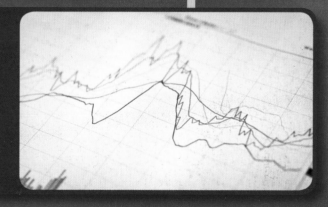

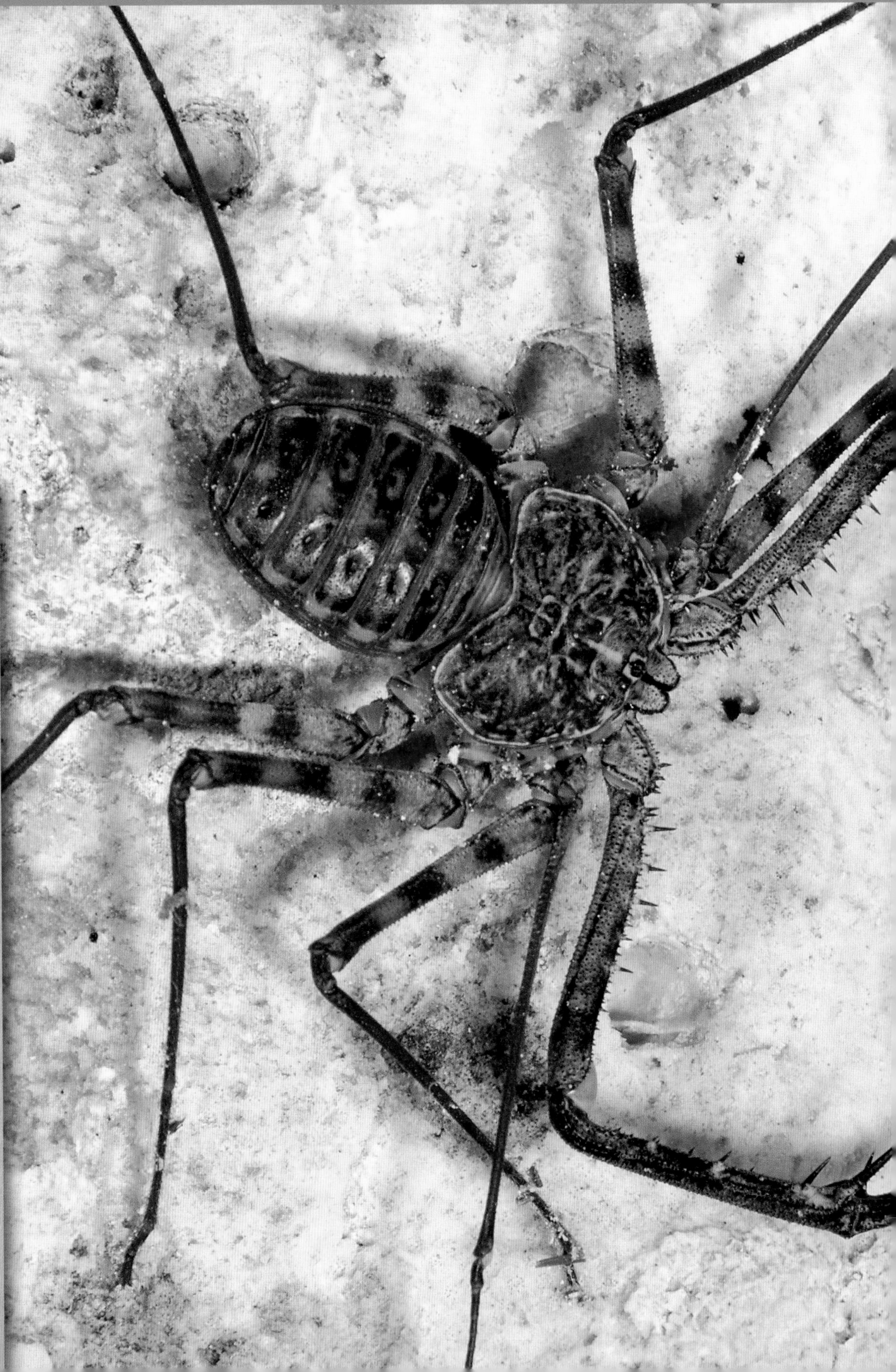

OTHER CREEPY-CRAWLIES

TOTAL SPECIES:
109,795

Arachnida
(uh-RAK-nuh-duh)
➡ Spiders
42,473 species

➡ Scorpions
1,947 species

➡ Mites
53,582 species*

➡ Ticks
891 species

Diplopoda
(duh-PLOP-uh-duh)
➡ Millipedes
7,753 species

Chilopoda
kye-LOP-uh-duh
➡ Centipedes
3,149 species

*Some scientists
think this is very
low and that there
could be more than a
million undiscovered
mite species.

Other Creepy-Crawlies

AT A GLANCE

Of the many animals that creep and crawl through the world, these insect cousins comprise more than 100,000 species. They are part of the same much larger group of animals as insects—they're arthropods. Like insects, these animals have legs with several joints, segmented body parts, and exoskeletons. Some experts believe there may be more than a million more yet to be discovered. These three classes of arthropod include both common and unusual creatures.

VARIEGATED WHIP SPIDER

Scientific name: *Damon variegatus*
Pronunciation: *DAY-mon vah-ree-uh-GAY-tus*
Legspan: Up to 8 inches
Habitat: Semi-arid savanna: sheltered rocky areas (including caves), tree holes, under tree bark
Food: Insects
Distribution: Eastern and southern Africa

FAST FACT The long front legs of this eight-legged creature are covered with sense organs. As it moves (sometimes sideways like a crab), those legs whip around, gathering information about its surroundings and possible prey.

Centipedes and millipedes are named for the impressive numbers of legs they have. (In Latin, *centi* means "100," *milli* means "1,000," and *pede* comes from the word for "foot.") These creatures live on the ground, in moist areas inside and outside. Centipedes eat insects, using poisonous claws near their mouths to stun or paralyze prey. They can attack and kill larger insects, birds, and even small rodents, amphibians, and reptiles.

Millipedes are scavengers that eat wood and decaying plant matter. Millipedes are slow-moving wanderers. They live among the soil, leaves, and plants on forest floors. Instead of mounting strong attacks, they rely on defensive moves. Millipedes can dig into the ground to escape, or roll into tight balls that make them hard to eat.

Millipede

Centipede

ONE PAIR OR TWO?

Centipedes have a pair of legs—one on each side—per body segment. Millipedes have twice as many.

Millipede

GIANT AFRICAN MILLIPEDE

Scientific name: *Archispirostreptus gigas*
Body length: Up to 15 inches
Habitat: Damp soil of forested areas
Food: Rotting plant matter
Distribution: Sub-Saharan Africa

FAST FACT This solitary creature is one of largest millipedes in the world.

WATCH OUT BELOW!

Centipedes move quickly, skittering across the floor or the soil to track down their fast-moving prey. They don't actually have 100 legs, as their name suggests. They can have from 15 to 300 pairs of legs. As they grow from birth, some species add segments and leg pairs until they reach their adult lengths. Centipedes eat insects, earthworms, spiders, and even lizards, shown here.

Their Best Feet Forward

Centipedes tend to have flatter bodies, and millipedes tend to be rounder. And millipedes have twice as many feet per body segment. Check out these many-footed arthropods to see if you can tell which is which.

SHOCKING PINK MILLIPEDE

Scientific name: *Desmoxytes purpurosea*
Body length: 1-1/4 inches
Habitat: Rain forest floor
Food: Rotting matter
Distribution: Thailand

FAST FACT Poisonous to eat, this millipede can spew the chemical cyanide when threatened. Its brilliant color is a warning signal to predators.

HOUSE CENTIPEDE

Scientific name: *Scutigera coleoptrata*
Body length: 1–1-1/2 inches
Habitat: Moist soil, indoors
Food: Insects, spiders
Distribution: North America, Europe, Asia

FAST FACT This centipede has exactly 15 pairs of legs as an adult. The rear pair is much longer than the others.

INSECTS AT WORK

Centipedes might creep you out if you see one on the floor or the wall, but they are helpful. They eat termites, spiders, bedbugs, and other pest insects.

DESERT MILLIPEDE

Scientific name: *Orthoporus ornatus*
Body length: 5 inches
Habitat: Desert areas
Food: Plant matter
Distribution: Southwestern United States, northern Mexico

FAST FACT By curling into a tight ball when threatened, this millipede protects its head and legs from attack, exposing a hard outer shell to the attacker.

FEATHER-LEGGED CENTIPEDES

Scientific name: *Alipes* (genus)
Body length: 5 inches
Habitat: Moist forest floor
Food: Insects, small arthropods
Distribution: Sub-Saharan Africa (also found in the West)

FAST FACT Named for its long, feathery back legs, this centipede rubs those legs to make sounds to warn off predators.

BLUE CLOUD FOREST MILLIPEDE

Scientific name: *Pararhachistes potosinus*
Body length: 2–4 inches
Habitat: High-altitude forest floor
Food: Rotting matter
Distribution: Mexico

FAST FACT This millipede shows off some of the brightest coloring among many-legged arthropods.

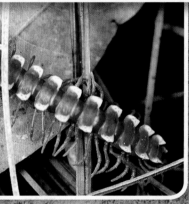

Spiders are not insects—they're arachnids *(uh-RAK-nids)*. With more than 40,000 known species, spiders come in an enormous variety of types around the world. But they all have some things in common. All spiders have eight legs and spin silk of some kind. And spiders have just two body parts—a cephalothorax (the front part, including the head) and an abdomen (the back part). Spiders do not have antennae or wings.

BUG BEHAVIOR

A spider's mouthparts include a pair of fangs that deliver venom into prey, which can range from insects to small mammals. The venom liquefies the prey's insides, and the spider slurps them up. Spiders inject venom by biting, and venomous wasps do so by stinging.

Tarantula

Black widows are easily recognized by the hourglass markings on the abdomens of the females, which are notorious for their poisonous bites. They eat insects and other arachnids, and the females are known for eating their mates. Their venom is considered to be more powerful than that of a rattlesnake.

BRAZILIAN WANDERING SPIDER

Scientific name:
Phoneutria nigriventer
Body length: 1-1/2–2 inches
Habitat: Higher-altitude rain forest
Food: Small animals
Distribution: Northern South America

FAST FACT The Brazilian wandering spider is thought to have the deadliest venom of any spider in the world.

Come Into My Web!

Perhaps the best-known behavior of spiders is their ability to spin webs. They eject silken threads from organs in their bodies called spinnerets. Different spider species use their silk in different ways—some use only single strands, while others create large, elaborate designs. Some young spiders spin out long strands of silk and use them like parachutes to move from place to place; this is called ballooning. Among spiders that spin webs, the webs' main use is for capturing prey. Depending on the spider, that prey can include almost any kind of small animal, from insects to birds.

WEB WEAVERS

While all spiders spin silk, different species weave different kinds of webs. Here are some examples.

Funnel-web spider
This spider gets its name from the funnel-like shape of its web. Some species in Australia have dangerous bites.

Trap-door spider
This spider weaves a thin web around the entrance to its burrow. Unwary prey become trapped in the net.

UNDERWATER LIVING

Spiders live in every type of habitat except the ocean—but there is a spider that makes an amazing home in water. The diving bell spider builds a web and fills it with air so it can breathe underwater. It can stay beneath the surface of a lake or pond for as long as a day.

Spiders come in a large variety of sizes, shapes, colors, and traits. Some are as small as 1/10 of an inch, while others can measure as much as 12 inches across. The smallest may be a rare spider found in Borneo called *Patu digua*. It's only about twice as big as the period at the end of this sentence. Here are some notable members of the spider family.

PASSIVE DEFENSE

Cobweb weavers weave some of the most recognizable webs, identifiable by their three-dimensional irregularity. The best known of this group are the dangerous widows, but the cobweb weaver shown here is harmless to people. In general, they are timid and curl their legs up in a ball when threatened.

GOLIATH BIRDEATER

Scientific name:
Theraphosa blondi
Body length: 12 inches
Habitat: Rain forest
Food: Small animals
Distribution: Northern South America

FAST FACT The Goliath birdeater is the heaviest spider, weighing about 6 ounces—that's the same as a newborn puppy. It has fangs nearly an inch long!

REGAL JUMPING SPIDER

Jumping spiders don't spin webs; they pounce on prey to capture it. Thanks to a system of hydraulics (energy from the movement of fluids) in their bodies, they can leap 20 times their body length. Add that ability to their nearly 360-degree vision, and jumping spiders have the tools to be powerful hunters. This is a regal jumping spider, one of more than 5,000 species in the jumping spider family, the largest family of spiders.

THAT'S FAST!

Huntsman spiders don't spin webs to capture prey—they don't need them. They hunt by running on their long legs, chasing down tasty insects such as cockroaches and small vertebrates. They are found in tropical areas, including Australia, Southeast Asia, the Mediterranean, South America, as well as in Florida and Hawaii.

After spiders, perhaps the next most-familiar arachnids are scorpions, with about 1,947 species worldwide. A scorpion is easily recognized by its upraised tail, at the end of which is a sharp stinger. It hunts spiders and insects, working only at night. It plunges its stinger into prey and uses large front claws to hold it still while feeding on its insides. Like spiders, scorpions have eight legs.

GIANT HAIRY SCORPION

Scientific name: *Hadrurus arizonensis*
Body length: 6 inches
Habitat: Desert areas
Food: Insects, invertebrates, small vertebrates
Distribution: Southwestern United States

FAST FACT This dangerous-looking creature is the largest scorpion found in North America.

BUG BEHAVIOR

Many species of scorpion, especially those that live in desert areas, glow when exposed to ultraviolet light. Scientists think proteins in their exoskeletons are reacting to the light. There does not seem to be a purpose for this trait—at least not one that has yet been discovered.

Italian scorpion
(Euscorpius italicus)

BABIES ON BOARD

Scorpion babies are born alive rather than in eggs. Their outer shells are very soft at birth. They stay with their mother, riding on her back, until they molt (shed their skin) and grow firm exoskeletons.

The arachnid world is varied, with many spiders, scorpions, and other eight-legged relatives. Here's a look at some of the many interesting arachnids.

GOLDEN WHEEL SPIDER

Scientific name: *Carparachne aureoflava*
Body length: 3/4 inch
Habitat: Desert
Food: Insects
Distribution: Northern Africa

FAST FACT When disturbed or being chased, this spider turns on its side and forms its legs into a circle. It then cartwheels down sand dunes to escape.

INSECTS AT WORK

Spider and scorpion venom is deadly to prey, and some is powerful enough to kill humans. However, it may help people one day. Scientists are studying spider venom as a potential treatment or cure for muscular dystrophy, strokes, and brain disease.

COMMON HARVESTERMAN

Scientific name: *Phalangium opilio*
Body length: 1/4 inch
Habitat: Tree trunk, forest
Food: Insects, decaying plants
Distribution: Global across Northern Hemisphere

FAST FACT Also known as daddy longlegs, these arachnids aren't spiders—they don't produce silk or weave webs. Daddy longlegs often cluster together in large groups.

DEER TICK

Scientific name: *Ixodes scapularis*
Body length: Less than 1/8 inch
Habitat: Grassland, forest
Food: Animal blood
Distribution: North America

FAST FACT These ticks spread the bacteria that cause Lyme disease, an infection that can make humans seriously ill or kill them.

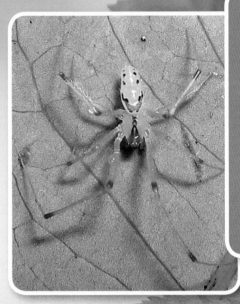

HAWAIIAN HAPPY FACE SPIDER

Scientific name: *Theridion grallator*
Body length: 1/4 inch
Habitat: Higher-altitude rain forest
Food: Insects
Distribution: Hawaii

FAST FACT The female of this spider is one of very few in the world that is an engaged mother. She cares for her spiderlings after they hatch, guarding them and bringing them food.

MIRROR SPIDER

Scientific name: *Thwaitesia argentiopunctata*
Body length: 1/10 inch
Habitat: Tree
Food: Insects
Distribution: Australia

FAST FACT The mirrorlike markings on this spider change in appearance, both over time and if the spider becomes agitated.

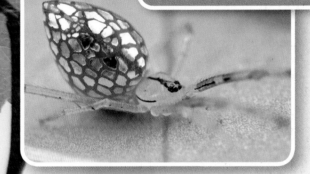

EIGHT-SPOTTED CRAB SPIDER

Scientific name: *Platythomisus octomaculatus*
Body length: 3/4 inch
Habitat: Rain forest
Food: Insects
Distribution: Singapore

FAST FACT This crab spider has a flattened abdominal section. To count all the spots, look on the underside for the eighth one.

SCABIES MITE

Scientific name: *Sarcoptes scabiei*
Body length: Less than 1/10 inch
Habitat: Mammal skin
Food: Mammal skin and fluids
Distribution: Global

FAST FACT Mites are the tiniest arachnids and are often nearly invisible without help from a magnifying glass. The scabies mite still makes its presence obvious, though. It tunnels into human skin, creating long marks that can be very itchy and can become infected.

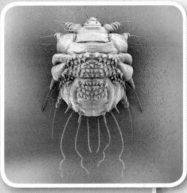

Insects in the News

Think we know all there is to know about insects? Think again! New discoveries are being made all the time, all around the world. Scientists working with insects have made discoveries that help people, help insects, and also raise new questions to investigate.

INNER GEARS

Humans invented gears to make machines work. The teeth of mechanical gears interlock to help machine parts move. In 2013, scientists looked at planthopper nymphs and discovered the first gears in the animal kingdom. The microscopic body parts look just like human-made gears. But the insects didn't come from a factory. The English scientists who found these planthoppers learned that the animals use their gears to make superquick hopping motions to escape trouble.

Gears in planthopper nymph body

ANTS AND CLIMATE CHANGE?

One of the biggest issues facing our planet's climate is the amount of carbon dioxide (CO_2) in the atmosphere. The more CO_2 in the atmosphere, the warmer the planet becomes. Scientists in Arizona have found that, in some cases, ants might help solve this problem. They found that having colonies of ants in a particular location reduced the amount of carbon dioxide more than 300 times when compared to places without ants. There is more to study on this subject, but with so many ants on Earth, this might be a big help someday.

WHAT'S THIS?

Does this show an alien invasion? No, but its shape is a clue to what is going on in this picture. This butterfly-shaped radar image is actually a huge swarm of monarchs flying over Missouri in 2014 while they migrated.

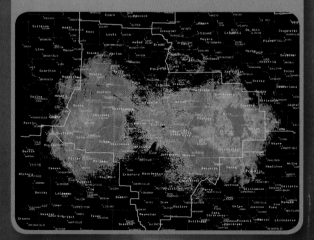

Scientists always look for answers. Whether using the latest technology, looking at things in a different way, or happening upon something new, they can uncover things earlier researchers missed...or simply couldn't see.

EUREKA!

When two different animals evolve the same small trait while living in different places, it's called convergent evolution. Insect experts found a prime example of this in Hawaii. On two separate islands, different types of cricket lost their ability to "sing." Why? The crickets were prey for a type of fly that listened for their song and then laid eggs on them. The fly larvae then attacked the crickets as parasites. If the crickets didn't sing, the flies couldn't find them, so they had a better chance of survival. Both types of flatwing cricket evolved this way on their own in separate locales, a rare example of convergent evolution.

GOING...GOING...GONE?

Imagine if more than half the cars in the United States disappeared. People would notice! This is what has happened to bees. In the past 50 years, the number of bees has dropped from 5 million to 2.5 million, according to the U.S. Department of Agriculture. Pesticides are one possible cause of what is known as colony collapse disorder.

HONEYBEE COLONIES
(IN THE MILLIONS) IN THE UNITED STATES

1960 5 MILLION

1970 4.2 MILLION

1990 3.4 MILLION

2014 2.5 MILLION

PUTTING SLEEPING SICKNESS TO BED

Tsetse flies live in Africa and spread the germs that cause sleeping sickness, which can be deadly to humans. In 2014, scientists unlocked the mysteries of the tsetse fly. After years of work, they found the fly's complete genetic code. Now that they finally understand how the insect's genes work, scientists hope to be able to control the spread of the flies in the future, which will prevent the disease from spreading, too.

Look and Learn

Reading about insects is fun, but doing activities or something creative with insects might be even more fun. Here are some ways that you can take your love of insects out into the world to learn more.

OBSERVE AND RECORD

If you'd like to record the types of beetles and other insects crawling around on the ground near your home, here's an easy way to catch them.

Make a pitfall trap.

1. Ask your parents for an empty tin can. It should be clean and dry.

2. Dig a hole deep enough to bury the can so that the rim is even with the soil level. (One good place would be near the garden—make sure your parents are okay with this.)

3. Put some rotting veggies in the bottom of the can to attract the bugs. You might put a piece of wood or foil-covered cardboard over the opening, at an angle so insects and air can get in but larger animals can't. The insects will come in for the food but will have a tough time climbing back out.

4. Check your trap daily and see what insects you caught, but don't pick them up because they might bite or sting. Be nice and release them back into the yard when you're done, though.

5. Keep a daily record of how many insects you trap and release, what they look like, and any other observations (such as the weather and the time of day you checked). Record keeping is an important part of any research project.

INSECT SUPER HERO

With their amazing strength, defenses, and ability to fly, insects would make great superheroes. Invent a new insect superhero. Model it after a particular insect or combine several insect parts. Is the hero big or tiny? Does it fly, or leap great distances like a grasshopper? Think about bugs that spew; can your hero use something like that as a weapon? After you've got a bug hero, invent a super villain that can be a worthy insect foe! You can do this by writing a story about your new hero or drawing a picture of it…or both!

SURVEY SAYS...

Entomologists and other scientists often take insect surveys, or counts. See how many different insects you can find in a survey of part of your yard or school yard. Here's how:

1. Mark out a square about 3 feet on each side. You can use string to make a boundary. Find a nice moist area of soil, perhaps with some grass or rocks that give the insects a variety of places to be.

2. Carefully look over every inch of the ground within the square.

3. Count how many bugs you see and note the numbers in a notebook. You can also write down what they look like, but don't pick them up—a cute-looking insect might actually be one that stings or bites.

4. Use a magnifying glass to make sure you find them all.

5. You can even dig into the dirt to find more.

6. Then you can expand the survey to different parts of the yard to find out where yet more types of insects live.

MACRO SNAP!

In some places in *Bugopedia*, you've seen super close-up images of insects. If you'd like to try making some yourself, there's an app for that! Most smartphones can use an app to help the camera take very close-up images. A regular camera may have a program setting for macro images, or a special macro lens. Here are some tips for close-up insect photography:

➡ Patience pays: Insects won't hang around waiting for you to take their picture. You might have to wait a while for just the right moment.

➡ Find cool colors: Look for contrast between the color of the insect and the color of the background. The animal will show up better that way.

➡ Hold still: Using a tripod or a monopod will help you focus better on your target.

➡ Prepare: What insects live near you? What plants do they feed on? Knowing these answers will help improve your chances of shooting amazing local insects.

PARTY TIME!

You can have a bug-themed party or after-school snack with these superfun ideas for sweet treats inspired by some of the insects in this book.

LADYBUG CUPCAKES FOR TWO

WHAT YOU'LL NEED:

- 2 unfrosted cupcakes
- 1 large tube of red icing
- 2 black gum drops
- 1 small tube of black decorating icing
- Chocolate drops or chips for spots
- 4 2-inch pieces of thin licorice strips

ANTS ON A LOG

WHAT YOU'LL NEED:

- Celery sticks
- Peanut butter (or soft cheese like cream cheese or cottage cheese)
- Raisins

An easy and fun treat!

1. Spread peanut butter (or cheese) in the celery sticks
2. Place raisins on top and enjoy.

This looks like it has a lot of steps, but if you use the photo as your guide, you'll make a cupcake almost too cute to eat!

For each ladybug cupcake:

1. Spread red icing on a cupcake.
2. Place a gumdrop at one edge flat-side down, for the head.
3. Put dots of red frosting on the gumdrop for the eyes.
4. Outline wings with the black decorating icing.
5. Use chocolate drops or chips to make the spots. Remember, ladybugs can have lots of spots!
6. Use thin licorice strips for antennae.

SOUNDING OFF

Insects can make a wide variety of noises. And so can you. Get a bunch of friends together (or just your family on your next car ride) and create an insect chorus.

What you'll need:
Index cards (one for each person)
Pencil, pen, or crayon

1. Write an insect's name and its sound on an index card. Repeat with other insects on the other cards. Or write the same insect's name on several cards if you want lots of people to make the same sound. Here are some suggestions to get you started:

➡ **Beetle:** *Click, click, click*

➡ **Bee:** *Buzz, buzz, buzz*

➡ **Cricket:** *Chirp, chirp, chirp*

➡ **Cicada:** *Hummmmmm*

2. Let each person pick a card (and a sound to make). Take turns making the sounds to create your favorite song. Or sound off together for a room (or car) full of insect tunes.

MAKE YOUR OWN INSECT

You know that insects have six legs as adults, antennae, and exoskeletons. Most also have wings. But, as you've read, there is still enormous variety in the insect world. Can you create an insect that is new to science? Combine the parts of insects you've learned about from *Bugopedia*: jointed legs, bodies in sections, wings, antennae, mouthparts, and more. You can draw your new bug, or use things like sticks, pipe cleaners, and various art supplies to make a model of it. Be creative! Nature has created millions of insects, but there's always room for one more.

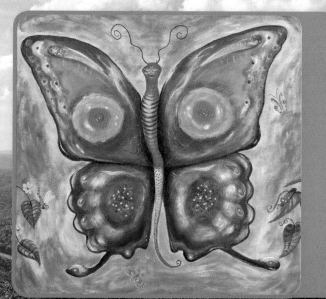

PLACES TO VISIT

CALIFORNIA

**California Academy
of Sciences**
Golden Gate Park
San Francisco, CA 94118
calacademy.org

*Visitors can go on an insect
scavenger hunt to find all the
places where insects are
featured in exhibits.*

**Natural History Museum
of Los Angeles County**
900 Exposition Blvd.
Los Angeles, CA 90007
nhm.org

*The zoo changes its
"residents" often, so you will
probably see new insects each
time you visit.*

ILLINOIS

The Field Museum
1400 S. Lake Shore Dr.
Chicago, IL 60605
fieldmuseum.org

*Examples from the insect world
make up half the museum's
entire animal collection.*

KANSAS

**University of Kansas
Natural History Museum**
1345 Jayhawk Blvd.
Lawrence, KS 66045
naturalhistory.ku.edu

*A great place for young people
to visit a good collection of
insects, many of which are
native to the Midwest.*

MASSACHUSETTS

**Museum of
Comparative Zoology**
Harvard University
26 Oxford St.
Cambridge, MA 02138
mcz.harvard.edu

*Exhibits at this museum are
changed often
to showcase an amazing
variety of insects, spiders,
and other creepy-crawlies.*

NEW JERSEY

**Insectropolis:
The Bugseum
of New Jersey**
1761 Rte. 9
Toms River, NJ 08755
insectropolis.com

*This entire museum is
dedicated to insects
and other arthropods.*

NEW YORK

**American Museum
of Natural History**
Central Park W. & 79th St.
New York, NY 10024
amnh.org

*This museum is home to 24
million insect specimens. Each
fall it hosts a special walk-in
butterfly exhibit.*

WASHINGTON, D.C.

**Smithsonian National
Museum of Natural History**
10th St. & Constitution
Ave. NW
Washington, D.C. 20560
mnh.si.edu

*On the second floor of this
museum, there is a special
exhibit called the O. Orkin
Insect Zoo, where you can see
hundreds of insects, spiders,
and other animals on display.*

CAMPING WITH BUGS

The Entomological Society
of America has a guide
on its website that gives
information about summer
bug camps in North America.
Camps are run by schools—
such as the University
of Georgia, Penn State
University, and the University
of California, Davis—as
well as by private groups in
Missouri; Toronto, Canada;
and other places. Visit
entsoc.org/resources/links/
entomology-summer-camps
to find out more.

INFORMATIONAL BOOKS TO READ

**Bugged: How Insects
Changed History**
Sarah Albee

Take a trip through time to find
out how insects and people
have connected in good ways
and bad through history. From
locusts to silkworms to the
bubonic plague, find out how
bugs have "bugged" us.

**The Case of the
Vanishing Honeybees:
A Scientific Mystery**
Sandra Markle

Colony collapse disorder is
causing real problems in the
bee world. This book takes a
look at the science behind the
issue and talks about what
people are trying to do to help.

**National Audubon
Society Field Guide
to North American
Insects and Spiders**

This book offers up-close
color photos of hundreds
of insects, plus detailed
descriptions of these and
many more. There's also
a handy pocket-size guide
with some of the most
often seen insects—
just right for backpackers
and insect spotters.

**Smithsonian
Handbooks: Insects**
George C. McGavin

America's top museum
put out this huge book that
covers insects, spiders,
scorpions, and more. There's
a companion handbook that
covers butterflies and moths
in great detail, too.

FICTION FAVORITES

Charlotte's Web
E. B. White

A thoughtful and loving spider
named Charlotte befriends
a pig named Wilbur. Her
marvelous webs help her
friend. This is one of the all-
time best children's books.

**Harry the Poisonous
Centipede's Big Adventure**
Lynne Reid Banks

Harry has to venture into
the big, wide, scary world
to help his friend.

**James and the
Giant Peach**
Roald Dahl

Escaping his wacky aunts,
James ends up inside a
giant peach, where he meets
a crew of fellow travelers,
many of whom are insects.

WEBSITES

www.entsoc.org

*This is the home of the
Entomological Society of
America. It includes news
about insect discoveries,
clubs you can join, and
even scholarships you
can apply for.*

**www.amentsoc.org/
bug-club/**

*The Amateur Entomologists'
Society website has a section
where kids can find out more
about insects; consider
joining their Bug Club.*

**kids.sandiegozoo.org/
animals/insects**

*The website of one of
the world's best zoos
features information about
the insects and other
arthropods that live at its
huge southern California site.*

Key: SS: Shutterstock, SU: Superstock, DR: Dreamstime, DC: Discovery Communications MP: Minden Pictures;
L: Left, R: Right, T: Top, M: Middle, B: Bottom, LtR: Left to Right: TtB: Top to bottom, C: Clockwise from top left

FRONT COVER: ©piotreknik/SS; BACK COVER: ©USGS; 1 BG: ©DC; 2-3 BG: ©schankz/SS; 4-5 BG: ©Gorawut Thuanmuang/SS; 6: ©Jim Heemstra; 7: ©Emilien Leonhardt/Hiroux Europe; 8-9 BG: ©SW_Stock/SS; 9 C: ©Marcel Span/SS, ©SW_Stock/SS, ©c photospirit/SS, ©DC; 10-11 BG: ©ANT Photo Library/Science Source; 12-13 BG: ©Science Channel/Alan Henderson/Discovery; 12 LtR: ©Yuangeng Zhang/SS, ©Tyler Fox/SS, ©Vitalii Hulai/SS; 13 TtB: ©Stephane Bidouze/SS, ©Ishbukar Yalilfatar/DR, ©THANAWAT TEAWPIYAKUL/SS; 14-15 BG: ©Triff/SS; 14: ©efendy/SS, 15 T: ©Abel Tumik/SS, B: ©Bershadsky Yuri/SS; 16-17 BG: blickwinkel/Alamy; 18-19 BG: ©Andreykuzmin/DR; 18 T: ©Tomatito26/DR, B: ©Henrik Larsson/SS; 19 TtB: ©FLPA/SU, ©Matthias Lenke/F1 ONLINE/SU, ©Joseph Calev/DR; 20-21 BG: ©Aliced/DR; 20 T: ©Rolf Aasa/DR, B LtR: ©Fedor Kondratenko/DR, ©Steve Gschmeissner/Science Source; 21 TtB: ©jupeart/SS, ©Claudio Divizia/SS, ©Melinda Fawver/SS; 22-23 BG: ©Klaus Reitmeier/SS; 22 T LtR: ©Charley Eiseman, ©Henrik Larsson/SS, M LtR: ©Henrik Larsson/SS; B LtR: ©VWPics/age fotostock/SU, ©Henrik Larsson/SS, ©Biosphoto/SU; 23 C: ©Mvuijlst at en.wikipedia [GFDL (http://www.gnu.org/copyleft/fdl.html), CC-BY-SA-3.0 (http://creativecommons.org/licenses/by-sa/3.0/) or CC BY-SA 2.5-2.0-1.0 (http://creativecommons.org/licenses/by-sa/2.5-2.0-1.0)], from Wikimedia Commons, ©Tomatito26/DR, ©Joseph Calev/DR, ©Pierre-Marc Brousseau, ©NaturePL/SU; 24-25 BG: ©photolinc/SS; 24 T R: ©Arto Hakola/SS, T L: ©Sue Robinson/SS, ©Henrik Larsson/SS; 25 T: ©Martin Fowler/SS, M: ©Bruno Kneubühler, B LtR: ©Dr. Morley Read/SS, ©Katarina Christenson/SS, ©Evgeniy Ayupov/SS; 26-27 BG: ©Triff/SS; 26 T L: ©Mau Horng/SS, all others: ©StevenRussellSmithPhotos/SS; 27 L TtB: ©wonderisland/SS, ©Napat/SS, ©PHOTO FUN/SS, R: ©Tomatito/SS; 28-29: ©Steven Deming/DR; 30-31 BG: ©James H Robinson/Getty, 30 L: ©NOAA/Joey Hulett, R: ©Mirko Zanni/Getty; 31 TtB: ©Juniors/SU, ©Greg Courtney, ©Charley Eiseman; 32-33 BG: ©Roman Kantsedal/DR; 33 T: ©Tomonishi/DR, B: ©Elliotte Rusty Harold/SS; 34-35 BG: ©Phurinee Chinakathum/DR; 34: ©Guy J. Sagi/SS, B LtR: ©Vishnevskiy Vasily/SS, ©Brian Lasenby/SS; 35: ©Viter8/DR, B LtR: ©EarnestTse/SS, ©Colette6/DR, ©Sarra22/DR; 36-37 BG: ©xfdly/SS; 36 T: ©Photo by Pierre Deviche; B: ©Brian Lasenby/SS; 37 T: ©Jessica Kuras/SS, M LtR: ©Photo by Pierre Deviche, ©Sfagnan/DR, B: ©maXx images/SU; 38-39 BG: ©pirtuss/SS; 38 T LtR: ©Elliotte Rusty Harold/SS; ©Doug Lemke/SS, ©Photographerlondon/DR, M LtR: ©Brian Lasenby/DR, ©Animals Animals/SU © By Vengolis (Own work) [CC BY-SA 3.0 (http://creativecommons.org/licenses/by-sa/3.0)], via Wikimedia Commons, B LtR: ©Laurie Knight/Getty, ©Gianluca Rasile/DR, ©Dave Montreuil/SS; 39 T: ©iliuta goean/SS, M LtR: ©Bonnie Taylor Barry/SS, ©imageBROKER/SU, ©Fotosutra/DR, B: ©Peter Schwarz/SS; 40-41 BG: ©Pakhnyushchy/SS; T LtR: ©Tyler Fox/SS, ©Craig Taylor/SS, B: ©Tony Campbell/SS, 41 L: ©Tomatito/SS, R: ©Jim H Walling/SS; 42-43 BG: ©Sofiaworld/SS; 42 T: ©NatalieJean/SS, B LtR: ©Pan Xunbin/SS, ©Joseph Parker and David Grimaldi/American Museum of Natural History, NY, ©Khomkrit Phonsai/SS; 43 T L: ©Attila Fodemesi/SS, B L: ©CHAINFOTO24/SS, R: ©alexsvirid/SS; B LtR: ©Tomatito/SS, ©Gallinago_media/SS, ©Jim H Walling/SS; 44-45 BG: ©littlesam/SS; 44: ©Nature's Images/Getty; 45 TtB: ©Gerry Bishop/Visuals Unlimited, ©jps/SS, ©Cuson/SS, ©Gilles Malo/DR; 46-47 BG: ©Jamesvancouver/DR; 46 TtB: ©photomatz/SS, ©Ivan Hor/SS, ©Ron Rowan Photography/SS, ©Adam Gryko/SS, 47: ©Guner Gulyesil/SS; 48-49 BG: ©Leela2414/DR, L T two: ©feathercollector/SS, B L: ©optimarc/SS, R: ©Mikhail Melnikov/SS; 49 L: ©PUMPZA/SS, R: ©Benjamin Simeneta/SS; 50-51 BG: ©ArtThailand/SS; 50: ©Roger Meerts/SS; 52-53 BG: ©Srinakorn Tangwai/DR; 52 L TtB: ©Dante Fenolio/Getty, ©Pan Xunbin/SS, ©AlessandroZocc/SS, ©Dr. Morley Read/SS, ©khazari/SS; R: ©Janette Asche/Getty; 53 T LtR: ©Gavin Parsons/Getty, ©James H Robinson/Getty, ©Kaipop/DR, B LtR: ©You Touch Pix of EuToch/SS, ©lertkaleepic/SS, ©Matt Howard/SS; 54-55 BG: ©imageBROKER/SU; 54: ©Marc Moritsch/Getty; 55 L to R ©NUM-Photo/SS, ©schankz/SS, ©Jose Angel Astor Rocha/SS; 56-57 BG: ©Jim Hughes/SS; 56 T: ©Aleksey Stemmer/SS, B: ©Nature's Images/Getty; 57 TtB: ©MP/SU, ©Michael McCoy/Getty, ©Andrew Burgess/DR; 58-59 BG: ©Pakhnyushchy/SS; 58 T: ©StockPhotoAstur/SS, B LtR: ©Steve Byland/SS, ©Xxlphoto/DR; 59 T: ©Ryan M. Bolton/SS, B LtR: ©Dreamman2008/DR, ©feathercollector/SS, ©Universal Images Group/SU; 60-61 BG: ©Natalia Gaak NWH/SS; 60 T: ©DC, B: ©Sebastian Janicki/SS; 61 T: ©WILDLIFE GmbH/Alamy, B two: ©MP/SU; 62-63 BG: ©4Max/SS; 62 T LtR: ©Aleksey Stemmer/SS, ©bikeriderlondon/SS, M LtR: ©ANT Photo Library/Science Source, ©DC, ©tea maeklong/SS, B C: ©Patricia Chumillas/SS, ©Dr. Morley Read/SS, ©DC, ©Alex Sun/SS; 63 T LtR: ©Peter Reijners/SS, ©MP/SU, M C: ©Piotr Naskrecki/MP, ©Michael D. Kern/naturepl.com, ©ZSSD/MP, ©MP/SU, B LtR: ©blickwinkel/Alamy, ©By Mydriatic (Own work) [GFDL (http://www.gnu.org/copyL/fdl.html) or CC BY-SA 4.0-3.0-2.5-2.0-1.0 (http://creativecommons.org/licenses/by-sa/4.0-3.0-2.5-2.0-1.0)], via Wikimedia Commons; 64-65 BG: ©Pakhnyushchy/SS; 64 T: ©blickwinkel/Alamy, B: ©enciktat/SS, 65 T LtR: ©Leena Robinson/SS, ©Joseph Calev/SS, B LtR: ©Barnaby Chambers/SS, ©Kristina Postnikova/SS; 66-67 BG: ©Dave Montreuil/SS, 67 T: ©Decha Thapanya/SS, B LtR: ©Pasi Koskela/SS, ©smuay/SS, ©thatreec/SS; 68-69 BG: ©Radu Bercan/SS; 68: ©Lodimup/SS; 69: ©National Oceanic and Atmospheric Administration/Dept. of Commerce; 70-71 BG: ©Education Images/UIG/Getty; 70 L two: ©irin-k/SS, M: ©Miramiska/SS, R: ©irin-k/SS; 71 T LtR: ©C.V. Riley/Library of Congress, ©Morphart Creation/SS, B LtR: ©Dimijana/SS, ©Sebastian Janicki/SS, ©Super Prin/SS, ©Peter Waters/SS, ©Sanit Fuangnakhon/SS; 72-73 BG: ©nineyoii/SS; 72 T: ©MP/SU, B: ©Bruno Kneubühler; 73 TtB: ©Joachim Bresseel, ©Alex Wild/Visuals Unlimited/Corbis, ©Bruno Kneubühler; 74-75 BG: ©mchin/SS; 75 T: ©wonderisland/SS, B LtR: ©encikAn/SS, ©Bettmann/Corbis; 76-77 BG: ©LeDi/SS; 76 T: ©Bernhard Michaelis/DR, B: ©NHPA/SU; 77 TtB: ©CSIRO [CC BY 3.0 (http://creativecommons.org/licenses/by/3.0)], via Wikimedia Commons, ©NHPA/SU, ©John W Bova/Getty; 78-79 BG: ©manzrussali/SS; 78 C: ©Alan Henderson/Minibeast Wildlife/Discovery, ©ikpro/SS, ©David Schleser/Nature's Images/Science Source, ©DC, ©Chantelle Bosch/SS, ©Digoarpi/DR ©MP/SU, ©EBFoto/SS; 79 T: ©Bruno Kneubühler, ©Bildagentur Zoonar GmbH/SS, ©Brian Maudsley/SS, M: ©Sebastian Janicki/SS, ©imageBROKER/SU, ©Nature's Images/Science Source, B: ©By Carrascal (Own work) [Public Domain] via Wikimedia Commons, ©Corbis/SU; 80-81 BG: ©Steve Gschmeissner/Science Source; 81 T: ©D. Kucharski K. Kucharska/SS, B: ©Alexandr Mitiuc /DR; 82-83 BG: ©lazlo/SS; 82 T LtR: ©Martin Dohrn/Science Source, ©By en:User:Ways [GFDL (http://www.gnu.org/copyL/fdl.html) or CC-BY-SA-3.0 (http://creativecommons.org/licenses/by-sa/3.0/)], via Wikimedia Commons, B LtR: ©Henrik Larsson/SS, ©MP/SU; 83 T L: © age photostock/SU, T R: ©Elliotte Rusty Harold/SS, B: ©USGS; 84-85 BG: ©K.Narloch-Liberra/SS; 84 L TtB: ©Hugo Darras, ©Nozomu Takeuchi (Chiba University), ©IrinaK/SS, R TtB: ©Nigel Cattlin/Science Source, ©David Pegzlz/SS, B LtR: ©YapAhock/SS, ©small1/SS; 85 T: ©Rimpilstilskin/DR, M: ©vblinov/SS, ©R.A.R. de Bruijn Holding BV/SS, B: ©Thierry Berrod, Mona Lisa Production/Science Source; 86-87: ©DC; 88-89 BG: ©costas anton dumitrescu/SS; 88 L: ©Kemal Taner/SS; R TtB: ©withGod/SS, ©Julia Kuznetsova/SS, 89 T LtR: ©Henrik Larsson/SS, ©Photographee.eu/SS, B LtR: ©Vincent S. Smith, ©George D. Lepp/Corbis; 90-91 BG: ©Voranat Rajchatan/DR; 90: ©Settawut Visedbubpha/DR; 91 T: ©Erni/SS, B: ©Radu Bercan/SS; 92-93 BG: ©2265524729/SS; 92: ©Fdelapena/DR; 93 L: ©muratart/SS, R: ©Mary Terriberry/SS; 94-95 BG: ©photolinc/SS; 94 TtB: ©Christian Musat/SS, ©Ed Phillips/SS, ©skynetphoto/SS; 95 T L: ©Igor Semenov/SS, T R: ©Roger Eritja/Getty, M: ©D. Kucharski K. Kucharska/SS, B: ©Millard H Sharp/Getty; 96-97 BG: ©Konjushenko Vladimir/SS; 96 C: ©Sandra Caldwell/SS, ©Paul Looyen/SS, ©Visuals Unlimited, Inc./Joe McDonald/Getty, ©age fotostok/SU, ©sergyiway/SS, ©Rbiedermann/DR, ©Oakdalecat/DR; 97 T LtR: ©Lcruise/DR, ©ChinKC/SS, ©Decha Thapanya/SS, ©PHOTO FUN/SS, M LtR: ©Biosphoto/SU, ©Yuangeng Zhang/SS, ©Darius Baužys/DR; B L: ©MP/SU, ©Stig Karlsson/DR, B R: ©Vilainecrevette/SS; 98-99 BG: ©USDA; 98: ©USDA; 99 T: ©Weldon Schloneger/SS, B: ©FLPA/SU; 100-101 BG: ©Ryan M. Bolton/SS; 100 T: ©Joseph Parker and David Grimaldi/American Museum of Natural History, B LtR: ©Eye of Science/Science Source, ©USDA ©Mark Bowler/naturepl.com; 102-103 BG: ©Ralph Loesche/SS; 102 T LtR: ©fivespots/SS, ©leungchopan/SS, B LtR: ©vladimir salman/SS, ©mexrix/SS; 103 T: ©olkapooh/SS, B LtR: ©Charles Brutlag/SS, ©Elena Elisseeva/SS; 104-105 BG: ©Serg Zastavkin/SS; 104 T: ©Henrik Larsson/SS, B LtR: ©Incredible Arctic/SS, ©Michael Wheatley/All Canada Photos/SU; 105 T LtR: ©Vladimir Wrangel/SS, ©Denis Burdin/SS, B LtR: ©mandritoiu/SS, ©PensiveDragon/SS; 106-107: ©James Jordan Photography/Getty; 106: ©Cathy Keifer/SS; 108-109 BG: ©PHOTO FUN/SS, 108: ©Eduard Kyslynskyy/SS; 109 TtB: ©Bahadir Yeniceri/DR, ©claffra/SS, ©Hwongcc/DR; 110-111 BG: ©irin-k/SS; 110 TtB: ©Stuart Wilson/Getty, ©erni/SS, ©Tips Images/SU; 111 TtB: ©Photo Researchers/Getty, ©Animals Animals/SU, ©Manuel Cayuela Lopez/SS, ©David Peter Ryan/SS; 112-113 BG: ©Yphotoland/DR; 112 T: ©Awgfoto/DR, B LtR: ©Photowitch/DR, ©Goran Turina /DR, ©Vaclav Volrab/DR; 113: ©Charley Eiseman; 114-115 BG: ©lola1960/SS; 114: ©Eric Isselee/SS; 115 T LtR: ©Liewwk/DR, ©Joel Shawn/SS, ©Henrik Larsson/SS, ©Kristian Bell/SS, M: ©kurt_G/SS, ©Stacey Ann Alberts/SS, ©Henrik Larsson/SS, ©Matt Gibson/SS, B: ©Bildagentur Zoonar GmbH/SS, ©Kenny Tong/DR, ©Lightboxx/SS, ©Pierre-Yves Babelon/SS; 116-117 BG: ©Oleksandr Lysenko/SS; 116 T: ©Hector Ruiz Villar/SS, B LtR: ©MartinMaritz/SS, ©Richard A McMillin/SS, ©George D. Lepp/Corbis; 117 TtB: ©Brad Steels/Alamy, ©Cosmin Manci/DR, ©MP/SU, ©Animals Animals/SU; 118-119 BG: ©Bildagentur Zoonar GmbH/SS; 118 T: ©Tzooka/DR, M LtR: ©Marek R. Swadzba/SS, ©Bruce MacQueen/SS, ©Hendroh/SS, B LtR: ©vblinov/SS, ©Vladimir Blinov/DR, ©Elliotte Rusty Harold/SS; 119 T LtR: ©Biosphoto/SU, ©Elliotte Rusty Harold/SS, M: ©Alan Henderson – Minibeast Wildlife, ©Ron Rowan Photography/SS, ©Suede Chen/SS, ©Alexander Potapov/DR, ©Ansis Klucis/SS; 120-121 BG: ©Louise Murray/Science Source; 120 L: ©Matt Edmonds, R TtB: ©M. Unal Ozmen/SS, ©Evgeny Karandaev/SS, ©mexrix/SS, ©dominique landau/SS; 121 T: ©Louise Murray /Science Source, B: ©Sofiaworld/SS; 122-123 BG: ©meunierd/SS; 122: ©USGS; 123 T: ©Trudy Simmons/SS, B: ©Nate Allred/SS; 124-125 BG: ©age photostock/SU; 124: ©Dennis van de Water/SS; 125 TtB: ©Legger/DR, ©Meryll/SS, ©Andreas Altenburger/SS; 126-127 BG: ©USDA; 126: ©Brandon Blinkenberg/SS; 128-129 BG: ©Decha Thapanya/SS; 128: ©Domiciano Pablo Romero Franco/DR; 129: ©smuay/SS; 130-131 BG: ©Steve Bloom Images/SU; 130 T: ©Radu Bercan/SS, B C: ©Jaco Visser/SS, ©Henrik Larsson/SS, ©ashkabe/SS, ©l i g h t p o e t/SS; 131 T LtR: ©MP/SU, ©EBFoto/SS, B C: ©Bruce MacQueen/SS, ©Han maomin/SS, ©Barry Blackburn/SS, ©successo images/SS, ©Henrik Larsson/SS, ©Guy J. Sagi/SS; 132-133 BG: ©Kumma/SS; 132 T and M L: ©MP/SU, M R: ©Parkpoom Photography/SS, B: ©Tony DiTerlizzi; 133 T: ©Jessica Kuras/SS, ©Csubick/DR, ©David Burke/DR; 134-135 BG: ©MP/SU; 134: ©Nigel Cattlin/Getty; 135 T LtR: ©Dr. Keith Wheeler/Science Source, ©CDC, M: ©Charles Mann/Getty, B: ©Michael De Nysschen/DR; 136-137 BG: ©Serg64/SS; 136 L TtB: ©Tom Burlison/SS, ©Tobyphotos/SS, ©chungking/SS, ©Marco Uliana/SS, M TtB: ©Cosmin Manci/SS, ©Aleksandr Kurganov/SS, ©ArtisticPhoto/SS, ©Iakov Filimonov/SS, R TtB: ©Peter Waters/SS, ©Raul Gonzalez Perez/Getty, B LtR: ©Petrov Anton/SS, ©Cosmin Manci/SS, ©Joseph Calev/SS, ©photonewman/SS; 137 T: ©Biosphoto/SU, B: ©John Cancalosi/Getty; 138-139 BG: ©Larry Keller, Lititz Pa./Getty; 138 T: ©Michael Warwick/SS, ©Martin Fowler/SS, ©ChrisTher Smith/DR; 139 LtR: ©Paul Reeves Photography/SS, ©James Urbach/SU, ©NHPA/SU; 140-141 BG: ©optimarc/SS; 140: L: ©Maria Dryfhout/SS, T R: ©Deming9120/DR, B R: ©Eduardo Grund/age fotostock/SU; 141 T: ©Jeffrey Coolidge/Getty, ©Melinda Fawver/SS; 142-143 BG: ©nooook/SS; 142 T L: ©Bahadir Yeniceri/SS, T R: ©Visuals Unlimited, Inc./Leroy Simon/Getty, B: ©MP/SU; 143 TtB: ©FineShine/SS, ©Martin Fowler/SS, ©By Charlesjsharp (Own work) [CC BY-SA 3.0 (http://creativecommons.org/licenses/by-sa/3.0)], via Wikimedia Commons; 144-145 BG: ©pirtuss/SS; 144 T LtR: ©Johan Larson/SS, ©hakoar/SS, ©John Anderson/DR, M: ©Jason P Ross/DR, ©Biosphoto/SU, ©NHPA/SU, B: ©Biosphoto/SU, ©Winelover/SS, ©Elliotte Rusty Harold/SS; 145 T LtR: ©NHPA/SU, ©MP/SU, M: ©Matt Jeppson/SS, ©Elliotte Rusty Harold/SS, ©Cheryl Davis/SS, B: ©Tomatito26/DR, ©alexsvirid/SS, ©Cathy Keifer/SS; 146-147 BG: ©iceink/SS; 146 T: ©Gil Wizen, B: ©D. Kucharski K. Kucharska/SS; 147 T: ©kurt_G/SS, B L: ©wonderisland/SS, ©sergyiway/SS, ©Phil Savoie/naturepl.com; 148-149 BG: ©Satoshi Kuribayashi/Nature Production/MP; 149 T two: ©Masato Ono, Tamagawa University, Tokyo; B: ©Lovely Bird/SS, ©Bruce Macqueen/DR, 150-151: ©MP/SU; 150: ©South12th Photography/SS; 152-153 BG: ©SARIN KUNTHONG/SS; 152 LtR: ©successo images/SS, ©AG-PHOTOS/SS, ©Nancy Kennedy/DR, ©MOSO IMAGE/SS, ©N Mrtgh/SS; 153 T: ©kurt_G/SS, B: ©Dr. Morley Read/SS; 154-155 BG: MP/SU; 154 LtR: ©Dr. Morley Read/SS, ©Hugh Lansdown/SS; 155 T LtR: ©Alex Wild, Inc/Visuals Unlimited/Corbis, ©D. Kucharski K. Kucharska/SS, ©Dr. Morley Read/SS, ©Mark William Penny/SS, ©Nathan Mlot and David Hu/Georgia Tech; 156-157 BG: ©TOM KAROLA/SS; 157: L: ©szefei/SS, R: ©Matthias Lenke/F1 ONLINE/SU; 158-159 BG: ©Joacquim F/Getty 158 LtR: ©Gerry Bishop/Visuals Unlimited, Inc./Getty, ©Amy White & Al Petteway/Getty; 159 T: ©Stephen Bonk/DR, B LtR: ©George Grall/National Geographic/SU, ©schankz/SS, ©Paco Toscano/SS; 160-161 BG: ©Jumnian Pelt/SS; 160 T L: ©Elliotte Rusty Harold/SS, T R: ©Bill Gozansky/age fotostock/SU, M: ©nrpphoto/SS, B: ©ex0rzist/SS; 161 TtB: ©Stig Karlsson/DR, ©John Cancalosi/Getty, ©Jonathan M. Yuschock; 162-163 BG: ©Bohbeh/SS; 162 C: ©Ajayptp/SS, ©noppharat/SS, ©DC, ©Alan Henderson/DC, ©NaturePL/SU, ©Timothy Lethbridge, ©Biosphoto/SU, ©FLPA/SU; 163 T LtR: ©William Radcliffe/SU, ©Acambium64/SS, ©Hakoar/DR, ©piotreknik/SS M: ©Elliotte Rusty Harold/SS, ©Katarina Christenson/SS, ©claffra/SS, ©DC, ©Trichopcmu/DR, ©Ly Min/SS; 164-165 BG: ©Steven Kutcher 164 T LtR: ©Science Source, ©Pascal Goetgheluck/Science Source, ©Alexander Raths/SS, B LtR: ©USDA, ©mertcan/SS; 165: ©Steven Kutcher; 166-167 BG: ©Juan G. Aunion/SS; 166 T: ©Jim Heemstra, B: ©Joel Ness; 167 T two: ©Joel Ness, B: ©donut8449/SS; 168-169: ©Ivan Kuzmin/SS; 170-171 BG: ©KampolG/SS; 170 T: ©Tim Hester/DR, B: ©Pan Xunbin/SS; 171 T: ©Tom Brakefield/SU, B: ©Universal Images Group/SU; 172-173 BG: ©Kritsada Namborisut/SS; 172 T: ©Chatchai Somwat/SS, B:©Animals Animals/SU; 173 T: ©Zack Frank/SS ©Piotr Naskrecki, ©Luis Stevens/Sierra, Mexico; 174-175 BG: ©Peter Taylor/DC; 174: ©Katarina Christenson/SS, 175 T: ©Jay Ondreicka/SS, B: ©Sinclair Stammers/Science Source; 176-177 BG: ©Antares614/DR; 176 L: ©MarkMirror/SS, R: ©zstock/SS; 177 T: ©Otto Hanh/Getty, B LtR: ©Roger Hall/SS, ©Matthijs Wetterauw/SS, ©John Pagliuca/SS; 178-179 BG: ©Scott Linstead/Science Source; 178 T: ©Eric Isselee/SS, ©MP/SU; 179: ©Hugh Lansdown/SS; 180-181 BG: ©Son Gallery/SS; 180: ©Audrey Snider-Bell/SS, ©FLPA/SU, ©DC; 182-183 BG: ©photolinc/SS; 182 T LtR: ©MP/SU, ©dirkr/SS, B: ©Aleksei Ruzhin/SS, ©Bruce MacQueen/SS; 183 T: ©Karl Magnacca, M and B L: ©Nicky Bay – sgmacro.blogspot, B R: ©Science Picture Co/SU; 184-185 BG: ©Sinelev/SS; 184 L TtB: ©Susan Robinson/DR, ©scigelova/SS, R TtB: ©Burrows and Sutton, University of Cambridge, UK, ©US National Weather Service, Saint Louis, Missouri; 186-187 BG: ©Iakov Kalinin/SS; 186 T: ©Blend Images/SS, B: ©DesignWolf/SS; 187 T: ©Auremar/SS, B: ©muratart/SS; 188 BG: ©Julia Ivantsova/SS; 188 L: ©Robyn Mackenzie/SS, R: ©Design Pics/SU; 189 T: ©Wiktoria Pawlak/SS, B: ©Melle V/SS

MEET THE MOST INCREDIBLE CREATURES

ON EARTH!

Learn everything there is to know about these awesome predators from Discovery™, the leading brand in nature programming!